SABRINA FISHER REECE

How to Balance Good and Evil

Understanding the Polarity of Human Nature and Choosing the Higher Path

First published by In59Seconds Publishing Co 2026

First edition

This book was professionally typeset on Reedsy.
Find out more at reedsy.com

This book is dedicated to every soul who has wrestled with their own shadow. We all carry light and darkness within us. There is no shame in that truth. The work is not to deny it, but to understand it, guide it, and choose wisely. May you learn to master what lives inside you, and walk the higher path with courage and compassion.

-Bri Reece

Contents

Introduction 1
1 The Choice You Make Every Day 5
2 The Personalities We Wear 14
3 Leading from the Hand or Leading from the Heart 27
4 The Power of Imagination and Choosing the Higher Path 34
5 Polarity Is the Design 46
6 The Daily Return to Light 57
7 What the Night Teaches 63
8 Our Daily Choice 67
9 Compassion in a World of Polarity 75
10 Emotional Control Is a Choice 83
11 The Discipline of the Higher Path 97
12 Choosing the Higher Side of Yourself 103
About the Author 108
Also by SaBrina Fisher Reece 111

Introduction

Most people have been taught to fear their darkness. From childhood, we are encouraged to identify with what is good, kind, loving, and acceptable, while anything angry, jealous, resentful, or destructive is pushed into silence. That silence does not eliminate those feelings. It only hides them. Pretending that the darker parts of our nature do not exist does not make us holy; it makes us unaware. Awareness is where the growth begins. There is nothing shameful about acknowledging that you are capable of both compassion and cruelty, patience and rage, generosity and selfishness. That capacity is part of being human. Identifying those opposites helps us to make conscious choices on how we want to show up in the world.

Human beings were born into a world governed by polarity. Day and night. Light and darkness. Heat and cold. Expansion and contraction. Inhalation and exhalation. High and low pressure systems. Positive and negative electrical charge. Life and death. These are not our opinions. They are observable structures woven into existence itself. Remove one side of these pairings and the system collapses.

Some opposites are not absolute in the same way. Up and down depend on orientation and human perspective. Right and wrong, as human language uses them, are often shaped by culture, experience, and moral frameworks. Those categories can shift depending on who is defining them. Natural polarities, however, do not change based on perspective. The sun will rise and set regardless of our opinion of it. The body will inhale and exhale without debate or instruction from us. Electricity will require positive and negative charge whether anyone agrees with it or not.

It would be unrealistic to assume that humanity somehow escaped this larger design. We are not separate from the grand structure of the universe. We are participants in it. Just as light and shadow coexist in nature, they coexist within each of us. Not as permanent labels, but as potential directions.

Many people prefer to call this dynamic good and bad. I often choose to call it light and shadow because it removes some of the emotional charge from the conversation. Light illuminates, clarifies, and warms. Shadow obscures, cools, and conceals. Both exist in nature. Neither makes the landscape defective. The issue is not the existence of shadow. The issue is what grows there when it is left unattended.

Polarity in the human being shows up as generosity and selfishness. Patience and impatience. Courage and fear. Compassion and indifference. Discipline and impulse. Integrity and deception. These are not abstract ideas. They appear in daily decisions. The presence of both capacities does not make you broken. It makes you responsible.

Free will was not given so we could deny one side of ourselves. It was given so we could direct and maintain control of ourselves. You were not designed to pretend the shadow side of you does not exist. You were designed to recognize it and choose how much authority it has over your behavior. Awareness is the bridge between instinct and intention.

Consider even the structure of your own body. The heart contracts and relaxes. Muscles tighten and release. The nervous system shifts between stimulation and rest. Blood sugar rises and falls within a regulated range. Balance is maintained through movement between opposites, not through elimination of one side. Health depends on regulation, not denial.

Weather systems follow similar patterns. Warm air rises. Cool air descends. Pressure differences create wind. Remove variation and the atmosphere would stagnate. Contrast produces movement and movement sustains life.

The same pattern applies internally. Emotional energy moves and anger rises. Calm returns and confidence builds. The question is not whether these states exist. The question is which ones you cultivate.

Understanding polarity this way removes shame from the conversation. It replaces denial with clarity. Light and shadow within you are not signs of moral failure. They are signs that you are human and alive within a structured universe. What defines you is not the existence of both. What defines you is your chosen direction over time. You cannot eliminate polarity or duality from creation. You can only learn to move within it wisely.

Every morning, when you wake up, you are positioned between possibilities. You always have a choice. You can lean toward bitterness or toward grace. You can feed resentment or cultivate forgiveness. You can move toward good health in your thoughts and habits, or you can allow neglect to quietly take root inside of you. These shifts are rarely dramatic. They unfold in conversations, in reactions, in private thoughts no one else hears. Our character is shaped in those subtle turns. The world does not simply happen to you; you participate in it through the direction you choose in every moment.

Understanding this changes everything. Darkness within you

is not a final verdict; it is a responsibility and a opportunity for growth. Denial it gives it more power. Shame completely buries it. But honest acknowledgment gives you authority over it. The goal is not to become divided, but to recognize the full spectrum of your nature so that your higher awareness can lead. When you accept that both capacities exist, fear begins to lose its grip. You begin to live consciously instead of reactively.

This book is not an accusation. It is an invitation to look inward without flinching, to understand the forces at work within you, and to realize that choosing the higher path is a daily act of intention. You are not defined by the existence of your shadow. You are defined by the direction you move.

"There is no need to destroy evil, it destroys itself when ignored" by Napoleon Hill

1

The Choice You Make Every Day

Life rarely presents itself as dramatic battles between heroes and villains. Most of the time, the tension between what we call good and what we call evil shows up in quiet, ordinary moments that no one else may ever see. Before we go any further, I want to gently address the word *evil* in the title of this book. I understand the weight of that word. For some, it carries deep pain. For others, it represents unspeakable acts that have forever changed their lives. If you have lost someone to violence, if you have experienced abuse, betrayal, or harm that shattered your sense of safety, I am not here to minimize that. There are behaviors in this world that are horrific. There are actions that cause devastation and trauma. Nothing in these pages is meant to excuse or dismiss that reality.

At the same time, I do not personally believe that God created anyone inherently evil. I believe we were created with free will. That gift of choice is powerful, beautiful, and at times dangerous. It allows us to love deeply, build families, create businesses, heal communities, and protect one another. It also allows us to act selfishly, destructively, or without regard for others. The word *evil* in this book does not label or judge a human being as irredeemable. It describes choices that move us away from our higher nature. It describes decisions that are not in our best interest or the best interest of those around us.

Men, women, and children all live within this polarity. No one is exempt from the internal tug-of-war between what society calls good and what society calls bad. That tension is not proof that you are broken. It is proof that you are human and that you have the ability to choose everyday. The ability to choose is not a curse. It is a gift and one of the greatest powers we possess. Every single day, whether in dramatic circumstances or in small unnoticed interactions, we are choosing direction.

The word *evil* in these pages speaks to the subtle decisions that either elevate your character or diminish it. It refers to the daily opportunity to act from kindness or from indifference, to simply be nice or mean. To act from integrity or from convenience, from patience or from irritation. These choices may seem small, but they accumulate. Over time, they shape your relationships, your reputation, your peace of mind, and ultimately the direction of your life. Each morning places you at the center of that decision. You begin choosing *Good or Evil* the moment you wake up in the morning.

You may see an elderly woman standing at the edge of a busy street, hesitating before stepping forward. You can keep walking, telling yourself someone else will help her, or you can offer your arm and guide her safely across. Neither option will make the evening news. One strengthens compassion; the other strengthens detachment. That is polarity in motion. That is character building in real time.

If you need an internal gauge, try this: if a thought, action, or response makes you feel loving, kind, compassionate, and at peace with yourself, it belongs in the good category. If it makes you feel small, ashamed, cruel, resentful, or filled with anger toward yourself or someone else, it leans toward the other side of the pole. That is your meter. That is your personal indicator. It is not about public opinion. It is not about what anyone else saw or approved of. It is about what happens inside of you.

This internal gauge is a positive thing. We need it in our lives. It is a built-in self-check that allows us to reel ourselves back in when we notice we are drifting toward meanness, indifference, harsh judgment, or lack of compassion. It is how we regulate ourselves without waiting for consequences to teach us a lesson. It helps us identify the areas where we still need to grow, not from shame, but from awareness.

Learning to use that gauge is vital, especially when it comes to how we treat ourselves. Many people are far more cruel internally than they would ever dare to be externally. If your self-talk is degrading, hopeless, or constantly critical, that also falls on the destructive side of the scale. Being harsh with yourself does not make you disciplined. It weakens your spirit. Just as we must learn not to act in ways that harm others, we must also learn not to mentally and emotionally harm ourselves. The same compassion you extend outward must eventually be extended inward. Honestly you should be kind to yourself first.

Here is a simple example: A self-checkout machine fails to scan an item in your cart. You notice it, and for a brief moment no one else does. You could say nothing and leave the store with something you did not pay for, quietly justifying it as a harmless oversight. You could also call the attendant over and correct it. No one applauds the honesty. No spotlight shines down. Yet in that private decision, you either reinforce integrity or erode it.

The direction matters, even when the dollar amount is small.

What matters even more is how you feel afterward. If you walk out with the unpaid item and feel a tightening in your chest, a drop in your spirit, a need to justify it, or a subtle sense that you betrayed your own standards, your internal gauge is speaking. If you correct the mistake and feel steady, clear, and aligned, that is also your gauge speaking. Over time, these small calibrations shape your character. They strengthen the part of you that wants to live upright and at peace.

This is not about perfection, It is about awareness. The goal is not to never drift toward irritation, selfishness, dishonesty or anger. The goal is to notice when you do, and gently guide yourself back. That internal meter is not there to condemn you. It is there to protect you and help you grow.

The holiday season creates its own quiet tests. Lines grow longer, the air feels heavier, and people's patience begins to wear thin. By the time you finally reach the front of the line, the cashier standing there may look drained. Her tone may be rude and abrupt or she simply may be overwhelmed and exhausted. In that moment, you can feel the pull to join the low murmur of complaints of the people in line behind you. It is easy to match their energy and respond with irritation. You could add your voice to the criticism and leave the interaction heavier than it already is.

But there is another choice available to you. You can choose not to participate in the negativity. You can decide not to add weight to someone who is already carrying too much. A genuine smile offered without sarcasm has more power than we realize. Speaking to her as a human being rather than a function behind a register shifts the entire interaction. A simple "Thank you for being here today" or a kind compliment about her effort or presence can soften something unseen. That single act may not change her entire day, but it changes yours. It strengthens empathy instead of resentment, and shows a positive example to the angry mob in line behind you. If even one other person is kinder to the cashier, then you have done your job. Kindness is not a performance, it is a conscious daily decision.

What happens internally matters even more than what you see externally. When you refuse to participate in negativity, you protect your own spirit. Instead of walking away irritated and justified, you leave feeling good about yourself. Compassion strengthens something inside of each of us, but resentment drains it. Every time you choose empathy over criticism, you are reinforcing the kind of person you want to become. That behavior is how the world changes for the better.

There is also a ripple effect that cannot be measured. The people in line behind you are watching, even if they pretend not to be. One softened interaction can interrupt the silent agreement that everyone must be harsh because the day has been hard. Even if only one other person decides to speak more gently to the cashier because of what they witnessed, something has shifted. A small act of grace and kindness has shifted the energy in the room. In a world that often feels tense and divided, choosing kindness in ordinary moments becomes a quiet form of leadership.

Sometimes the choice is even more personal. A friend is sick, and you do not feel like making the call. You are tired yourself super busy. You would rather rest, and calling to check on them may lead to a long phone call. But reaching out requires an effort that you would want someone to make for you. Silence requires absolutely nothing. Deciding to check in anyway shifts something inside you. It trains your heart to move toward connection instead of convenience. It builds the habit of caring when it would be easier not to.

None of these moments involve extreme wrongdoing. They involve guided, conscious intention and direction. Moving toward kindness, honesty, responsibility, and compassion strengthens one side of your nature. Moving toward selfishness, indifference, dishonesty, or hostility strengthens the other. Over time, the repeated tilt in one direction shapes your identity. You are not defined by a single misstep, nor are you transformed by a single generous act. You are shaped by patterns. You have the free will to show up anyway you chose in this world. Why not develop habits that allow you to chose the higher path one moment at a time.

We are all here trying to be good, live better, enjoy this life experience and find peace. The best way to navigate this life in my opinion is to attempt to put out exactly what you want back in return and when you don't simply start over again the next day with love and patience for yourself. We are all a work in progress.

Understanding this removes unnecessary shame while increasing accountability. Having the capacity to be unkind does not make you a terrible person. Having the impulse to take what is not yours does not make you irredeemable. Those impulses reveal that you are human. What defines you is how you respond to them. Recognizing the pull does not weaken you; it gives you the opportunity to choose consciously.

Polarity exists whether you acknowledge it or not. Ignoring it does not remove it. Denying your darker impulses does not eliminate them. Bringing awareness to them allows you to guide them. Each day offers countless chances to move slightly upward in character or slightly downward in consciousness.

Those movements are subtle, almost invisible, but they are powerful.

As we close this first chapter, I want you to understand something clearly: this book is not here to point fingers at you. It is not here to shame you for the moments you lost your temper, spoke too quickly, shut down emotionally, or chose wrong when you knew better. It is here because you are human. I am guilty of traveling to the bad side of the pole myself. That is why I am writing this book. Every one of us has stood in that space between two choices and felt the pull in both directions. That does not make you broken. It makes you human and aware.

There is no judgment here. If anger lives in you, you are not alone. I suffered with anger issues for many years. If jealousy has surfaced in you, you are not alone. If you have made decisions you regret, spoke to someone in a rude offensive way, you are not by yourself. We have all been there. The presence of those impulses does not define you. What defines you is your willingness to look at them honestly and decide who you want to become moving forward. Growth begins the moment you stop pretending you are only light and start taking responsibility for how you handle the shadow.

Balancing what we call good and evil is not about becoming a perfect person. It is about becoming conscious of your behavior. It is about recognizing that every day you wake up with power in your own hands. You have the power to heal or the power to harm. The power to speak life over yourself and others or the power to tear everything down. We all have the power to forgive or the power to hold grudges which can cause sickness and disease. You will not always get it right. None of us do, but what matters most is that you keep choosing and trying again and again. That you keep returning to the higher path when you drift away.

If you are reading this, it already means something inside of you wants to grow into a better person. That desire alone tells me there is goodness rooted deep within you. There is truly goodness within us all. Over the next chapters, we are not going to deny the darker side of human nature, nor are we going to let it run our life. We are going to understand it and learn from it. We are going to use it as information to help us become the best version of ourselves.

You are not your worst thought, action or reaction. You are a person with the ability to choose again tomorrow morning. That ability is sacred, and it represents hope.

You wake up in the center of that polarity every single day, with the freedom to lean in either direction. The side you consistently choose shapes the person you inevitably become.

GOOD
EVIL
Kind
Cruel
Patient
Impatient
Honest
Dishonest
Generous
Selfish
Compassionate
Indiffecent
Courageous
Fearful

2

The Personalities We Wear

Healing is a journey and it rarely begins gently. When I first stepped into my spiritual journey, I was not soft, open, or ready to be transformed. I was mad at God and very wounded. Trauma has a way of hardening the edges of your personality, especially when you have survived more than you have processed. The pain I experienced from witnessing the murder of my grandmother shaped me into someone who knew how to protect herself by hardening her heart, but I did not yet know how to release that hardness and allow love back in. The abandonment I felt from my mother only deepened that armor. Those two experiences taught me, at a very young age, that life could change in an instant and that the people who are supposed to stay in our lives sometimes leave.

I did not fall apart under the weight of that pain; I adapted to it. I built walls. I convinced myself that if I did not get too close to others I would not be hurt. I tried to protect my heart and prevent more pain. Somewhere along the way, that protection became my priority, and emotional distance felt safer than vulnerability. I trained myself to stay guarded, to measure how much of myself I revealed, and to maintain control in every situation so that no one could catch me off balance again. That posture passed for strength. People saw independence, ambition, and discipline. They saw a woman who could handle her business and did not need anyone to rescue her. What they could not see was the constant calculation happening beneath the surface, the quiet belief that closeness was dangerous and that love always carried the risk of sudden loss.

Self-sufficiency became my shield, but it was rooted in fear rather than freedom. Opening my heart fully felt reckless because experience had already taught me how quickly life can shift and how suddenly something precious can be taken away. Trust felt naïve to me at the time, dependence felt like a setup for disappointment, and emotional restraint felt like wisdom. I truly believed that keeping myself composed, guarded, and slightly detached was maturity. What I did not understand then was that I was confusing protection with peace.

Without consciously deciding to do so, I built a life structured around minimizing risk, especially emotional risk. I kept parts of myself reserved. I loved people, but carefully. I showed up, but with an invisible boundary that said, "Do not come too close." That strategy did reduce the likelihood of being blindsided by heartbreak, but it also quietly reduced joy, intimacy, and the depth of connection I truly longed for. The very walls I constructed to survive what had already happened to me were now standing in the way of the life I said I wanted to live.

My friend Beau was the one who first introduced me to a self-help seminar called CEC. At that point in my life, I was functioning, successful, and disciplined. On paper, everything looked solid. I had built a business, maintained structure, and carried myself with consistent strength. What most people could not see was how emotionally guarded I had become. Success does not automatically equal healing. Discipline does not mean softness. Beneath the surface, I was still carrying grief, disappointment, and betrayal that I had never fully processed.

CEC was a five-day intensive seminar held in a hotel, where a collective group of facilitators and psychologists worked closely with participants to uncover emotional patterns and buried wounds. I did not walk into that ballroom searching for comfort. I walked in with my defenses fully intact. The wall I carried had taken years to build. It had protected me when I needed protection. It had helped me survive heartbreak and navigate life without collapsing. What I did not yet understand was that the same armor that once saved me was now preventing me from healing.

My arrival was not marked by eagerness or surrender. I came to the seminar very guarded, observant, and slightly defiant, unsure whether anyone in that room could access a place inside me that I had worked so hard to seal shut. Skepticism felt safer than vulnerability. I listened carefully, but I kept my emotions contained. I was determined not to be easily impressed or emotionally exposed.

The leader of the seminar, a man named Sam from Iran, carried a presence that was calm, direct, and steady. His demeanor did not demand attention, yet it commanded respect. I watched him closely, still skeptical, still measuring the environment, still unwilling to fully let my guard down. At that time, I believed I was simply being strong. In reality, I was standing in a room designed for transformation while gripping tightly to the very shield that was keeping me from it.

During one exercise, we were asked to walk in a circle to

beautiful music while the panel observed us. They had been studying us for three days, watching how we spoke, how we reacted, how we carried ourselves. One by one, participants were pulled from the circle and assigned three personalities that the facilitators believed they embodied. We were told to go to a store, find costumes, and return prepared to demonstrate those three identities in front of the group. The experience felt theatrical and uncomfortable, yet I agreed to participate.

The first personality they gave me was Heidi Fleiss. Instead of feeling insulted, I understood the connection immediately. As the owner of Braids by SaBrina in Los Angeles Ca for thirty years, employing more than 1,700 women in the community, I knew how to lead, command, and organize. Heidi Fleiss was known as a madam and businesswoman. I recognized that assertive, no nonsense side in myself. Putting on a black jacket and carrying a small black book was easy. That part of me was familiar and comfortable.

The second personality surprised me. They assigned me Etta James. A long gown and a soulful song were required. Softness, vulnerability, emotion. Those qualities did not feel as natural at the time. My exterior was firm. I carried an attitude that said I did not need anyone's help and no one better no try to bond with me emotionally. The seminar cost two thousand dollars, and my attitude about the cost was simple. If nothing changes within me from the seminar, the only thing lost is money. Opening up emotionally was not something I did easily. Seeing Etta James in myself felt confusing because I had not allowed that tenderness to surface in those early days of the program.

The third personality stunned me completely. They chose Cupid. What? For Me? Cupid was a symbol of love, connection, and affection. The only African American woman in the room, surrounded by people of different nationalities, I had not been especially warm or inviting. I was not cruel, but I was definitely distant. Smiling did not come naturally in unfamiliar environments, and trust did not come quickly. The idea that these facilitators could look at me and see Cupid felt almost absurd. I could not understand how they had witnessed love shining through someone who was working so hard to appear guarded.

Returning to perform those three personalities changed something inside me. Playing Heidi Fleiss was effortless. Embodying Etta James required me to soften. Stepping into Cupid forced me to confront a truth I had tried to hide. No matter how tightly pain wraps around you, it does not erase your capacity to love. That side may be buried, but it does not disappear. As I stood there performing Cupid, emotion overtook me. The group responded with warmth and affection. Hugs came from people I had barely spoken to. They told me they saw my strength, but they also saw my heart. Being embraced by individuals from backgrounds different than my own softened something I had kept rigid for years.

Another exercise required small groups to solve a problem collectively. Irritation surfaced quickly when my team struggled to find direction. Without being appointed leader, I stepped into that role naturally. Orders were given by me to them and my instructions were very clear. So clear that we solved the problem in record time. I was now the default leader so I was the one who spoke and delivered the correct answer to the problem they gave us to solve. We had all found the correct solution collectively, and when we presented it to the panel, they applauded the accuracy. Their response did not end there though. They acknowledged the solution, then pointed out that it had been delivered it and forced everyone to find the solution through my Heidi Fleiss personality. We had the right answer but the task was not complete yet. They sent us back with a new requirement. I was to keep my role as leader and guide the team to solve another problem, but this time operate from Cupid.

That moment reshaped my understanding of polarity within myself. Strength was not the issue. Leadership was not the issue. The tone and energy behind it were the issue. The same outcome could be reached without aggression. Authority did not require me to be so harsh. Confidence did not require me to be so intimidating. Returning to the group and guiding them from a place of encouragement and love rather than force produced the same correct answer, yet the atmosphere felt completely different. Best lesson I ever learned.

For years, therapists and well meaning people in my life had encouraged me to discard that harder side. They suggested I eliminate it entirely because it did not serve me well in my relationships with others. The seminar offered a different perspective. The hardened personality had been built for survival. They helped me understand why the harder side of me was created. It protected me when I needed protection. Survival mechanisms are not flaws; they are responses to pain. Removing them entirely is unrealistic and unnecessary. During the seminar a facilitator explained it in a way that stayed with me forever. That personality is like a coat. There may be seasons when you need to wear it. Cold environments require protection. The mistake is wearing that heavy coat every single day, even when the weather has changed.

Learning that I did not have to destroy that hardcore side of myself, but rather control when and how I used it, was liberating. The Heidi Fleiss in me did not have to disappear. She simply did not need to run my entire life. Etta James and Cupid were not fantasies; they were real aspects of who I was. The revelation was not that one side was good and the other evil. The revelation was that all three existed within me. Choice determined which one showed up.

That seminar was the best two thousand dollars I ever spent because it taught me something no one had explained before. You can reach the same destination through different expressions of yourself. Results do not justify harshness, and power does not require coldness. Strength does not cancel out softness. The goal is **Not** to erase parts of your nature. The goal is to become conscious enough to decide which side you are leading with.

Polarity lives inside you whether you acknowledge it or not. Growth begins when you stop pretending you are only one thing and accept that we all have light and dark within us. Each day we rise is a new opportunity to chose which is leading us.

Polarity lives inside you whether you acknowledge it or not. Growth begins the moment you stop pretending you are only light or only shadow and accept that both exist within every human being. There is nothing shameful about that truth. The presence of darkness does not make you defective. It makes you responsible. Each day you wake up is another opportunity to decide which part of you will take the lead.

You do not have to be afraid of the darker impulses that surface at times, in yourself or in others. Anger, jealousy, pride, selfishness, and fear are signals, not life sentences. They are invitations to become more aware, not evidence that you are a terrible person. Pretending they do not exist only gives them more control. Looking at them honestly gives you the power to change them. Awareness is not condemnation. It is maturity and growth.

You do not have to be afraid of the darker impulses that surface at times within yourself or in others. Anger, jealousy, pride, selfishness, and fear are signals, not life sentences. They are invitations to become more aware, not evidence that you are a terrible person. Pretending they do not exist only gives them more control. Looking at them honestly gives you the power to change them. Awareness is not condemnation. It is maturity and growth.

There is deep freedom in being able to say, "Yes, that thought crossed my mind," or "Yes, I felt that reaction rise up in me," and then choosing differently anyway. That is strength in its truest form. That is character being built in real time. Darkness only becomes dangerous when it operates without your awareness. Once you can see it clearly, name it without shame, and redirect it with intention, it begins to lose its authority over you.

A few years ago, I experienced something that tested everything I teach in my books. I went on a nationally televised court show. The case itself was solid. A former client tried to scam me out of nine thousand dollars, and when the facts were presented, the judge saw right through it. I won the case fair and square. I walked out of that courtroom feeling proud of how I articulated myself and confident that truth had prevailed. I had on a beautiful designer suit. I was calm, composed, and grounded. I spoke articulately and confidently. I won, she did not get a dime. I flew home and that was that.

Months later, when the episode aired, I was not prepared for what came next. The world did not focus on the victory. They did not comment on the eloquent way I handled myself. They did not mention the fact that I had defended my integrity fairly and successfully. Instead, they zeroed in on my hair. Apparently, the hairstyle I chose exposed thinning around my hairline. I have always had high self-esteem, so it never even crossed my mind that it would become the headline. Yet that is what people latched onto.

The woman who lost the case was angry. Instead of accepting the ruling, she launched an all out cyber-bullying campaign against me. Clips of the show began circulating online with comments dissecting my appearance. Strangers who knew nothing about me felt bold enough to criticize my hair, my hairline, and my looks. Every time I opened my phone, someone had tagged me or sent me another post. Thousands of insults poured in.

It hurt, no doubt it was painful to endure. I am strong, but I am still human. Reading comment after comment about something so personal chipped at me. There were moments when I wanted to fire back, matching evil for evil and cruelty for cruelty. There were moments when sarcasm sat on the tip of my tongue. There were moments when pride whispered that I should defend myself aggressively and put people in their place.

That was the pole of polarity right in front of me. That was the choice. that we are faced with during times like this. I could have responded from the wounded part of me, the part that felt exposed and embarrassed. I could have thrown insults back. I could have allowed anger to justify cruelty. Instead, I made a decision that even surprised me. I responded to many of those comments with kindness. I even created a #JustOneDayOfKind ness Movement. I have a video on Youtube entitled "Just One Day of Kindness" by SaBrina Fisher Reece. I reminded people that while I could withstand it, there are young women and men who cannot. There are people who have taken their life for less.

I pointed out that cyber-bullying destroys people's self-esteem and unfortunately sometimes costs people their lives. I refused to become what they were projecting onto me.

That was not easy mentally and emotionally. It was one of the hardest emotional disciplines I have ever practiced.

Privately, people would inbox me and say they admired how I handled it. They applauded the positivity, but rarely in public. That, too, was revealing. The world often feels safer tearing someone down than standing up for someone who chooses love and kindness. Still, I was proud of myself. My self-esteem took big a hit, yes it did, but my emotional maturity grew. I saw clearly how quickly the darker side can be activated when ego feels attacked. I also saw how powerful it is to choose differently.

That experience showed me something profound about the personalities we wear. Under pressure, the mask slips. The version of you that responds when you are criticized, embarrassed, or wounded reveals what you have truly cultivated inside. Anyone can be kind when they are praised. Character shows itself when you are mocked.

There is deep freedom in admitting, "Yes, I wanted to clap back," or "Yes, I felt the sting," and then consciously choosing not to let that pain dictate your behavior. That is strength. That is emotional authority. Darkness only becomes dangerous when it operates unconsciously. Once you see it rising in you and you still decide to move toward the higher version of yourself, it loses control.

Every sunrise carries a quiet mercy with it. When the light breaks through your window in the morning, it is not asking who you were yesterday. It is not replaying your worst reaction or holding you hostage to a moment when you lost your temper, doubted yourself, or responded from a place of hurt. A new day does not erase what happened, but it does offer you space to respond differently. The direction you lean when you become aware of yourself is what shapes your character, not the mistake you made before you understood better. Patience is still available even if rage showed up yesterday. Compassion is still within reach even if you were sharp with someone you love. Integrity is not canceled because ego spoke too loudly last week. The opportunity to shift toward your higher self remains open for as long as you are breathing.

Carrying both light and shadow inside you does not make you defective. It makes you human. Everyone you admire, everyone you look at and think has it all together, is managing that same internal battle. The personalities we wear are influenced by pressure, environment, exhaustion, insecurity, and old wounds that have not fully healed. The work is not to pretend the darker impulses do not exist. The work is deciding which version of yourself you will strengthen through repetition. One reaction does not define you. One harsh comment from someone else does not define you. Even a painful thought that crossed your mind in a weak moment does not define you. What defines you is the pattern you choose to build. What defines you is which side of yourself you consistently feed.

Over time, those repeated choices become identity. The personality you practice under stress becomes the one that shows up automatically. If you nurture awareness, discipline, and compassion, that is what will surface when life tests you. If you indulge resentment and pride, that is what will take the lead. The power in this realization is that nothing about you is fixed in stone. You are not sentenced to an old version of yourself. Growth is available as long as you are willing to look inward honestly and choose intentionally.

As this chapter closes, I want you to feel relief, not pressure. You are not being judged here. You are being invited. Invited to notice the masks you wear, the reactions you default to, and the stories you tell yourself about who you are. Invited to understand that you are not trapped by your past behaviors. You are becoming something every single day. The question is not whether light and shadow exist within you. The question is which one you will strengthen through your choices.

Tomorrow morning when you open your eyes, the decision will be waiting quietly again. Not dramatic and loud. Just present, and you will have the authority to decide the type of person you want to be.

THE PERSONALITIES WE WEAR
Kind
Angry
Brave
Fearful
Grateful
Jealous

3

Leading from the Hand or Leading from the Heart

Polarity does not only show up in quiet personal decisions. It reveals itself in leadership, in parenting, in business, and in every position where influence exists. Looking back over the decades I spent building Braids by SaBrina, I can clearly see how both strength and impatience shaped the environment I created. My intentions were pure. My heart wanted freedom for the young women who worked beside me. My methods, however, were sometimes driven more by urgency than by softness.

From the age of twenty-six to fifty-six, I built what became my golden goose. That salon was not just a business. It was proof that a young Black woman from difficult beginnings could create stability and wealth with her own hands. I made an absolute fortune in that industry, and I was proud of it. Beneath that pride was something deeper. I did not want another young Black girl to struggle the way I had. I did not want them dependent on public assistance, unstable relationships, or survival-based decisions. I wanted them financially literate. I wanted them secure. I wanted them powerful.

So I taught them what I knew about business. I taught them how to braid professionally and run a salon like a structured business. I took them to the bank and made them open accounts. As I learned I shared the information with them. I sat them in front of my financial advisor so they could hear, sometimes for the first time, that putting away twenty-five dollars a month could change their future. The knowledge was solid and valuable. My intention was always love. But I was a Leo alpha female so the delivery was not always gentle. I knew I had a responsibility to share the knowledge but I had no idea how to share it softly.

At that stage of my life, I led with authority. I worked seven days a week. I was always tired. I was responsible for payroll, rent, utilities, inventory, and the livelihood of multiple families. When you carry that kind of weight, patience can wear thin. I believed pressure produced results because pressure had shaped me. Survival had made me sharp. It had made me decisive. It had made me strong.

Strength, however, sits right next to harshness on the polarity scale. Leadership can build or intimidate. Protection can slide into control. I was not cruel, and I was never careless, but I can admit now that sometimes my ruling hand spoke louder than my nurturing heart.

There was one particular season when I had about eleven employees working under me. Business was booming, money was flowing, and the salon was full. At the same time, my staff was unruly. One employee in particular tested my limits daily. She was consistently late. Her hygiene was poor. Customers had quietly complained about her attitude. I tried to correct the behavior privately more than once.

Eventually, I called a staff meeting. My intention was to address the overall atmosphere without singling anyone out.

I spoke in general terms about professionalism, punctuality, respect for customers, and pride in presentation. I was trying to keep it balanced. I was trying not to embarrass her.

Instead of receiving the message quietly, she began making snappy comments under her breath. She rudely talked back and interrupted me with sarcasm. She challenged my authority in front of the entire team. Something in that moment shifted inside of me.

I remember it vividly as if it was yesterday. Her whole body seemed to illuminate in red. That is the only way I can describe it. It was as if my vision changed. My anger rose so fast it startled even me. In that split second, I wanted to grab the heavy decorative statue that sat on my desk and hit her with it. That thought flashed through me like lightning.

That was polarity. That was the pole I speak of. That was the exact space between good and evil, the play where you choose.

I was nowhere near the spiritual seeker and teacher I am today. I had not yet done the deep internal transformation work. Still, something inside me knew that crossing that line would destroy everything I had built. One violent reaction, one two-second loss of control, could have ended my business, my freedom, and my reputation. I stepped back physically. I felt the heat in my body. I felt the surge of adrenaline. I felt the rage. Then I made a choice, and I fired her immediately.

It was never about hatred. I loved her dearly. She had worked for me for ten years off and on, and there was history there. It was not about humiliation either. The decision to fire her came from a much deeper understanding. Anyone who could push me that close to losing control did not belong in my space, no matter how long we had known each other. In that moment, I recognized that my livelihood mattered more than my pride. Protecting the business I had built required restraint, not retaliation. Choosing self-regulation over reaction was not weakness; it was strength.

Learning how to balance good and evil does not mean you will never feel anger. It does not mean you will never have the urge to shake someone, raise your voice, or slam your fist on a desk. Anger is often impulsive and untamed, a surge of energy that rises quickly and demands expression. That energy, by itself, is not evil. The capacity to feel anger is part of being human. What matters is how you handle it. What matters is what you choose to do with that surge once you recognize it.

Anger can either push you toward destruction or become a signal that something needs attention. The direction you take in that moment determines where you move along the pole. Even at the height of frustration, the simple act of pausing and acknowledging what you are feeling creates space. In that space, you regain authority. You may feel as though you have lost control, but the very awareness of your anger means you still have a choice. You can pull yourself back. You can redirect that energy. You can choose the higher side of yourself, even when the emotion feels overwhelming.

There are thousands of people sitting in jail cells right now because of a two-second decision. A punch thrown in pride. A weapon grabbed in rage. A car accelerated in revenge. Those moments are rarely planned. They are reactions. In those flashes of intensity, polarity presents itself clearly. One side says pause. The other side says act now.

Self-regulation is one of the greatest gifts you can teach yourself. It will protect your relationships. It will protect your finances. It will protect your reputation. It will protect your freedom.

Getting angry does not make you a bad person. Wanting to retaliate does not mean you are broken. Feeling the surge of fury does not cancel out your goodness. The shadow exists in all of us. Pretending it does not is naïve. Learning to govern it is maturity.

When I look back at that salon meeting, I do not shame myself for feeling what I felt. I honor myself for what I chose. That decision strengthened something inside me. It proved that even without formal spiritual training, I possessed the ability to step away from destruction.

Leadership, like life, is full of these moments. A disrespectful tone. A missed deadline. A betrayal. A public challenge. Every time, the pole stands in front of you. React impulsively and risk everything. Respond strategically and preserve your power.

Balancing good and evil in daily life is not about erasing the darker impulses. It is about understanding that they are signals, not commands. Anger may signal that a boundary has been crossed. Disrespect may signal that an adjustment is needed. The higher path does not require silence or submission. It requires measured action.

Firing that employee was not revenge. It was regulation. It was me choosing not to allow her behavior to pull me into a version of myself that would have cost me dearly. Sometimes the higher path means walking away. Sometimes it means removing someone from your environment. Sometimes it means saying no without violence.

As I matured, I realized that patience could accomplish what pressure once did. Authority did not have to be loud to be effective. Respect did not have to be demanded; it could be cultivated. I began leading with more balance, more awareness, more emotional control.

That salon taught me more than how to braid hair and run payroll. It taught me how quickly polarity can surface under stress. It taught me that exhaustion weakens emotional filters. It taught me that self-regulation is not optional for leaders. It is essential.

The woman who wanted to throw that statue and the woman writing this book are the same person. The difference is awareness and practice. You do not become good by pretending you have never felt dark impulses. You become stronger by recognizing them and choosing wisely anyway.

Do not beat yourself up because anger exists in you. Do not shame yourself because sometimes you want to react. Instead, train yourself. Pause. Step back. Breathe. Walk away if necessary. Fire the employee. End the meeting. Leave the room. Protect your future.

That is what it means to understand polarity. That is what it means to balance good and evil. It is not perfection. It is a conscious daily choice.

#In59Seconds

4

The Power of Imagination and Choosing the Higher Path

In order to experience the best life has to offer, you must first believe that the best is possible for you. You must believe you deserve it. That belief does not begin in the external world. It begins in the mind. Imagination is one of the greatest gifts given to humanity. It is a creative force. It allows us to see something internally long before it ever appears externally. When understood correctly, imagination becomes a tool for choosing the higher path within the polarity of human nature.

Every thought you hold forms a picture in your mind. Whether you realize it or not, you are constantly imagining outcomes. If the images you rehearse are filled with love, success, health, and peace, you are strengthening the light within you. However, if your imagination repeatedly plays scenes of failure, rejection, loss, betrayal, or disaster, you are feeding the shadow side of your internal polarity. The imagination does not judge. It simply creates. The responsibility lies with you and in what you choose to create.

Many of us spend a surprising amount of time imagining

what we do not want. We picture businesses failing. We see relationships ending. We imagine being embarrassed, rejected, or left behind. Fear quietly uses imagination as its canvas. When that happens, we are participating in the darker side of our internal polarity, not in the dramatic sense of evil, but in the sense of choosing thoughts that diminish our power instead of strengthening it.

Understanding how to balance good and evil begins here. Instead of imagining lifelong loneliness, picture yourself deeply loved, sitting across from a partner who respects and cherishes you. Rather than rehearsing the collapse of your business, envision celebrating fifteen years of success surrounded by friends and family who admire your talent and perseverance. The higher path is not denial. It is you choosing a deliberate direction.

You create your lived experience through the thoughts you consistently hold. Having a negative thought does not make you bad. It makes you human. Recognizing it is where growth begins. The presence of darkness or shadow within you is not the problem. Allowing it to dominate your mind without question is the problem.

I often teach a phrase in my motivational videos that I call "Catch and Cast" or "Recognize, Reject, Replace." The first step is awareness. Notice the negative thought. The second step is consciously reject the thought. Refuse to allow that thought to rule your emotional state. The third step is replacement. Replace the negative thought with a positive one. Insert a better, stronger, more empowering thought in its place. Mastering this practice is how you govern the polarity within yourself.

I have had simple moments in my life that illustrate this clearly. One afternoon, my two youngest daughters and I were driving home from shopping. My ten-year-old mentioned that she needed to complete homework in Google Docs. I use Google Docs to write my books. I casually responded that she should create her own account because I did not want anything happening to my un-finished books. She has a habit of creating accounts and forgetting passwords. That one comment triggered a mental movie inside my mind. I imagined her accidentally accessing my account and deleting important manuscripts. Within minutes, I was angry over a situation that had not happened.

The entire ride home I felt myself becoming more upset. My body responded as though an actual loss had occurred. I created it all in my mind. A possibility that never even happened. I had to stop and speak to myself internally. "She didn't even do it. This did not happen." That was a moment of self-regulation. I was choosing whether to let an imaginary scenario pull me toward anger or to redirect myself toward reason. Nothing had taken place. The suffering was entirely self-generated. Many of us are guilty of this. Creating drama and unnecessary suffering in our head for no reason.

This is how polarity operates quietly within us. The tension is not always dramatic for others to witness or loud. Often it shows up in the private theater of the mind, where we create worst-case scenarios that never materialize and react emotionally to stories we invented ourselves. The body responds as if the danger is real, heart rate rising, muscles tightening, mood shifting, all because the imagination wandered into fear. It is possible to suffer deeply over something that has never happened and may never happen. That kind of suffering is avoidable when we learn to guide our imagination instead of allowing it to drag us wherever it chooses to go.

The imagination itself is not the problem it is not the enemy. Misuse of the imagination is. The imagination itself is one of the greatest gifts we have been given. Albert Einstein once said, *"Imagination is more important than knowledge. Knowledge is limited. Imagination encircles the world."*

That same power that allows humanity to invent, to create art, to design cities, and to build businesses also allows us to imagine rejection, betrayal, and catastrophe. The imagination itself does not carry a moral charge. It is not inherently positive or negative, righteous or destructive. It is simply a faculty of the mind, a creative instrument capable of generating images, possibilities, and outcomes. Like any powerful instrument, it reflects the intention of the one using it. The direction is what determines whether it builds or destroys.

When imagination is left unchecked, it tends to drift toward fear because fear is loud and urgent. When imagination is directed intentionally, it strengthens faith, resilience, and possibility. Napoleon Hill wrote, "*Whatever the mind can conceive and believe, it can achieve.*" That principle does not apply only to success in business or wealth. It applies to peace of mind as well. If you continually conceive of disaster, your nervous system will live as though disaster is imminent. If you deliberately picture solutions, growth, and protection, your body and spirit begin to operate from steadiness instead of panic.

The Divine Creator gave us free will, and part of that free will includes authority over our mental focus. We cannot control every external circumstance, and life will still present loss, disappointment, and uncertainty. What we can control is how we interpret what is happening and how far we allow our imagination to run ahead of reality. The quality of your daily experience is deeply connected to the images you rehearse in your mind. When imagination becomes disciplined rather than reactive, polarity begins to balance. Fear loses some of its volume and your faith grows stronger. The same mind that once created internal chaos becomes the instrument that creates calm.

Keep in mind, your imagination can bring your negative thoughts into reality as well. Try not to spend an extended amount of time imagining bad things. When you notice that you are daydreaming and it's not a good dream, stop it in its tracks and intentionally imagine something that makes you happy. We have so many unfounded subconscious fears that we don't realize how much we sit and think about things like death, car accidents, heartache, etc. Make sure your positive thoughts outweigh your negative. God gave us the power to bring things into existence. Make sure the things you bring into your life are good things.

Once you finally accept you do have this power, you will be more mindful of monitoring your thinking patterns. I can't say it's easy to continuously monitor your thoughts, but it will prove to be worth the effort and eventually it will become easier to do. Anything you do daily will become a habit. It should be everyone's goal to make positive thinking a habit.

Consider the quiet times you have to just sit and breathe and access your thoughts as a gift, because a gift is exactly what these moments are; a wonderful opportunity to take charge and be solely responsible for your happiness. We spend years blaming others for how our lives turn out, but rarely do we take responsibility for not making use of our divine God-given power to design a better life. Accepting this power does not negate the hurt that we have suffered at the hands of others. It doesn't erase injustices or minimize inequalities in the world. It simply frees us from the bondage of being a victim to the pain and trauma we have endured for the rest of our lives.

Despite the title of this book, I don't actually believe in classifying people as good or bad because both negative and positive qualities exist within all of us. However, the remarkable power to create and manifest our desires is not reserved only for those the world perceives as good. Mind Magic is available to everyone. Each of us has the ability to use it in constructive ways or in destructive ones. What matters is remembering that human beings are subject to certain immutable laws. If you use this power to create chaos, harm, or ill will, the consequences will inevitably return to you. The principle of like attracting like is a universal law of karma that operates whether we acknowledge it or not. In simple terms, the energy you send into the universe will find its way back to you. For that reason, it is important to pay attention to how much time and focus you devote to imagining negative outcomes, especially when you are upset with someone and find yourself dwelling on thoughts of their downfall or misfortune. What you project outward does not simply disappear. It circles back, and many traditions say it returns multiplied.

The goal is not to eliminate imagination but to recognize it for the extraordinary gift that it is and learn to elevate it. Instead of repeatedly rehearsing disasters in your mind, rehearse resilience. When your thoughts drift toward anger and humiliation, redirect them toward strength and kindness. When the mind begins to picture abandonment and fear, replace that image with stability, love and security. Imagination will always be active because it is part of human consciousness, but the direction it takes is something you can influence. The real choice lies in whether your imagination serves your higher nature or feeds the darker impulses that live in the shadows of the mind. That is where polarity truly exists, not in the absence of thought and imagination, but in the direction and intention behind them.

There was a period when I began receiving citations from the City of Los Angeles for parking my H2 Hummer on my lawn. I had owned that property for more than twenty years, and that truck was not just a vehicle to me. I purchased it in 2003 when Hummers were first released and paid full price for it, proud of what I had accomplished at that stage of my life. Even after it became inoperable and sat on the grass for years with dry-rotted tires, I could not bring myself to sell it. It represented a chapter of success and independence. When the citations started arriving in the mail, it felt intrusive and personal. During a casual conversation, a neighbor suggested that someone else on the block must have called the city to complain, and instead of questioning that assumption, I accepted it immediately as fact.

Once I embraced that story, my entire perception shifted. I began scanning the street differently. The same neighbors who had waved at me for years suddenly became suspects in my imagination. I replayed scenarios in my mind of one of them dialing the city, filing a complaint, and pretending to smile in my face the next morning. I convinced myself that someone who greeted me warmly had betrayed me behind my back. Without any confirmation, without any proof, I internally declared war on all of them. Every time I drove down the block, I looked at houses with suspicion. Every wave felt fake. Every greeting felt staged. Meanwhile, the people I had mentally accused continued their routines, completely unaware that I had assigned them the role of enemy in a story that existed only inside my head.

When I reflect on that period now, I can almost laugh at

how much emotional energy I wasted. I was fighting from every direction, north, south, east, and west, and I was the only soldier on the battlefield. It never occurred to me in those early moments that a city inspector could have simply driven by, noticed an inoperable vehicle sitting on grass for years, and enforced a regulation. There very well may have been a legitimate ordinance I had ignored. The neighbors I silently resented had no idea I was even upset. They were living their lives while I was building a case against them in my imagination. The suffering I felt was real, but it was self-inflicted. It was born from assumption, fed by repetition, and strengthened by my refusal to pause and question my own narrative.

This is what mental self-torment looks like in everyday life. No one attacked me. No one confronted me. No one even said an unkind word. Yet I allowed resentment to take root because I chose to believe a version of events that justified my anger. Each time I repeated the story to myself, my body reacted as if the betrayal had truly occurred, tightening and bracing as though the threat were real. The emotional tone shifted almost immediately, my thoughts grew sharper and more defensive, and a sense of calm slowly slipped away. Nothing had changed outside of me, yet internally there was real turmoil unfolding.

That is how powerful unchecked imagination can be. It can create enemies where none exist and manufacture pain out of thin air. The lesson in that season was not about parking regulations or city citations. It was about recognizing how easily the mind can turn uncertainty into accusation and how quickly we can begin punishing ourselves over stories we never verified.

Balancing good and evil in daily life often looks like this. It looks like interrupting suspicion before it hardens into bitterness. It looks like choosing peace instead of ego. The thoughts you entertain determine the emotional climate you live in.

Imagination can also elevate circumstances beyond logic. I could have taken a few minutes, closed my eyes, and imagined receiving a letter from the city waiving all the fees. Instead of rehearsing hostility, I could have rehearsed resolution. "All things are possible" is something I say all the time, it is not naïve optimism. It is alignment with possibility instead of fear.

Miracles fit into this conversation as well. Many claim to believe in them, yet when something extraordinary happens, logic rushes in to dismiss it. One day in 2023, my daughters and I were driving down Slauson Avenue in Los Angeles. All the traffic lights were out at a major intersection that had previously been the site of a fatal accident involving six lives. As we approached, anxiety surfaced. With the lights out in every direction, the risk felt high. I began praying aloud for protection and safe passage for everyone present.

Right in the middle of that prayer, before we reached the center of the intersection, the traffic lights turned back on. There had been no police intervention yet. They simply activated. It was our turn to cross. I looked at my daughter in disbelief. That moment felt miraculous. Whether someone chooses to label it coincidence or divine intervention, I know what I experienced.

Driving has long triggered anxiety in me. Fearful imagination is something I have had to work on consistently. I cannot allow myself to dwell on images of catastrophic accidents. That mental discipline is part of choosing the higher path within polarity. After a tragedy like the Nicole Linton accident, fear can easily dominate thought patterns. However, even from catastrophe, growth can emerge. If an event causes people to drive more cautiously, then some measure of good has been drawn from a horrific situation.

Another moment confirmed this for me. One rainy afternoon, after explaining to my daughters that even when a light turns green you should pause and look both ways, I modeled exactly that behavior. I paused. I looked right, then left, and proceeded. A vehicle sped through the intersection at an unbelievable speed, water spraying from its tires. I pressed the gas instinctively. Somehow, impossibly, the car missed us entirely. Logic struggles to explain how. Faith accepts protection.

In moments like that, polarity becomes tangible. Life and death exist side by side. Human control and divine intervention intersect. Free will operates, yet grace intervenes. My role remains the same. I must continue choosing awareness, caution, and faith rather than living in constant fear.

Imagination can create torment, or it can cultivate faith. It can build resentment, or it can construct reconciliation. It can rehearse disaster, or it can prepare success. The mind is a battlefield where good and evil are rarely dramatic. They are subtle. They are thought by thought.

When you understand polarity within human nature, you stop being surprised by the presence of shadow. Instead, you focus on governing it. You choose the higher interpretation. You redirect the mental movie. You discipline your imagination. You align your thoughts with the life you want to experience.

If you can imagine destruction, you can imagine healing. If you can imagine betrayal, you can imagine loyalty. If you can imagine loss, you can imagine restoration. The imagination is neutral. Your direction determines whether it strengthens darkness or light.

Commit to spending time intentionally imagining the life you desire. See peace. See restored relationships. See financial stability. See health. See harmony. When negative scenarios attempt to dominate, catch them, reject them, and replace them. That is how you balance the polarity within yourself.

Miracles may not always be as dramatic as traffic lights turning on or speeding cars missing your vehicle by inches. Sometimes the miracle is simply catching a destructive thought before it becomes a destructive action. Sometimes the miracle is choosing not to wage war on neighbors in your own mind. Sometimes the miracle is choosing to calm yourself before anger spills into a relationship.

Choosing the higher path is rarely loud. It is internal and deliberate. It should be something you repeat daily.

If you can imagine it wisely, you can move toward it intentionally, and that is how we balance good and evil.

Kind
Brave
Grateful
Angry
Fearful
Jealous

5

Polarity Is the Design

Understanding polarity begins with observation. It does not require advanced theology or complex philosophy. It requires paying attention to how the world actually functions, and how we react to it. Opposites are not rare interruptions in creation. They are the structure of it. Positive and negative charges govern electricity. North and south poles define magnetism. Expansion and contraction regulate breathing. Action and reaction shape physics. High pressure systems move against low pressure systems to create weather patterns. The entire natural world operates through complementary forces interacting with one another.

Science does not argue against polarity and duality; it documents it. Electricity flows because of the relationship between positive and negative charges. Remove one and current stops. Magnetism depends on opposing poles that cannot exist independently. Every magnet, no matter how small, carries both a north and a south pole. Attempts to isolate one pole result in the immediate reappearance of the other. The structure refuses singularity. The design insists on complement.

Day and night provide one of the clearest examples of this rhythm. The Earth rotates on its axis approximately every twenty four hours, creating alternating periods of light and darkness. This cycle regulates circadian rhythms in human beings and animals alike. Hormones shift according to light exposure. Melatonin increases when darkness falls, encouraging rest. Cortisol rises with morning light, preparing the body for activity. Removing either half of the cycle creates imbalance. Constant daylight disrupts sleep patterns and mental health. Unending darkness produces similar distress. Life depends on both phases.

The sun setting is not a flaw in creation but a necessary occurrence within a larger system of balance. Crops require periods of darkness to complete certain biological processes, and soil benefits from the cooling hours of night when temperatures drop and ecosystems are able to regulate themselves. Even the human nervous system depends on this same rhythm. Continuous stimulation eventually exhausts it, while periods of rest restore its function and stability. When productivity continues without pause, breakdown becomes inevitable. This cycle of activity and recovery reflects intention rather than accident, and it unfolds without any human involvement or management. The processes that sustain life on Earth operate in sequence and in harmony long before human beings interfere with them or attempt to understand them. This book is not written to convince you that God exists, but it is difficult to ignore that a power greater than us governs the patterns that sustain the natural world. The order present in these systems points toward something responsible for their design and continuity, something that exists independent of human action or approval.

Evidence of this same principle appears throughout the natural sciences, where balance is consistently maintained through opposing forces working together. The human body preserves homeostasis by constantly adjusting between internal conditions that move in different directions. Blood sugar rises and falls within controlled limits throughout the day, body temperature shifts slightly as the body regulates itself, and muscles contract before releasing again to create movement. Even the heartbeat depends on alternating electrical impulses that travel through the cardiac muscle in a precise sequence. Remove that alternating pattern and life stops immediately. What we call polarity is therefore not a philosophical idea or abstract theory. It is a biological reality that operates inside every living organism and within every system that supports life on this planet.

Physics describes the universe in terms of forces interacting. Newton's third law states that for every action there is an equal and opposite reaction. That principle governs motion from the smallest particle to the largest celestial body. Gravity pulls downward. Momentum pushes forward. Resistance creates stability. Without opposing forces, structure collapses. Stability is not achieved by eliminating opposition but by balancing it.

These scientific realities mirror a spiritual truth. If polarity is woven into the physical universe, it would be illogical to assume human nature stands outside that design. Emotions rise and fall. Thoughts shift between optimism and doubt. Desire competes with discipline. Compassion can coexist with irritation. The human psyche reflects the same structural duality found in nature.

Creation, as described in scripture, begins with separation of light from darkness. The narrative does not eliminate darkness.

It assigns it purpose. Evening and morning form a complete day. Darkness is not described as evil in itself; it is described as part of order. Light illuminates. Darkness restores. Together they create rhythm.

Human beings were granted free will within that framework. Choice exists because polarity exists. If only one direction were possible, morality would lose meaning. The presence of options gives weight to decisions. Moving toward patience instead of anger carries significance precisely because both are available. Choosing honesty over deceit matters because deceit is an accessible alternative.

Polarity does not imply equal moral value. Light and darkness in nature are complementary. Kindness and cruelty in human behavior are not morally equivalent. Recognizing the presence of darker impulses does not glorify them. It simply acknowledges their reality. Awareness prevents self deception. Denial strengthens what remains unexamined.

Psychological research supports the idea that suppressed impulses often resurface in distorted ways. Studies in behavioral science show that emotional repression can increase stress responses and reactive behavior. Individuals who refuse to acknowledge anger are more likely to express it unconsciously through passive aggression or withdrawal. Integrating awareness of difficult emotions reduces their destructive impact. Integration requires honesty.

The design of the brain itself reflects dual processing. The prefrontal cortex governs reasoning and impulse control. The amygdala processes fear and emotional reactivity. Both structures serve survival. Acting purely from the amygdala produces chaos. Ignoring emotional signals entirely creates disconnection. Healthy functioning depends on communication between the two. Rational thought and emotional awareness must coexist.

Historical spiritual traditions across cultures recognize this dual structure within humanity. Eastern philosophies describe yin and yang as complementary forces interacting dynamically. Western theology discusses flesh and spirit. Modern psychology speaks of conscious and unconscious processes. Different languages describe the same pattern. Humanity contains tension between higher awareness and lower impulse.

Observing societal trends also reveals polarity. Crime rates rise in environments of scarcity and trauma. Communities with increased access to education and stable support systems demonstrate lower levels of violent behavior. Statistical analyses consistently show correlations between early childhood adversity and later behavioral issues. This does not excuse harmful acts. It highlights roots. Darkness in behavior often emerges from unhealed wounds rather than inherent monstrosity.

The presence of trauma does not remove responsibility. It explains context. Polarity within human behavior reflects both innate capacity and environmental influence. Individuals choose responses within circumstances. That choice may be constrained by conditioning, yet it remains significant. Growth requires acknowledging both impact and agency.

Economic systems reflect dual forces as well. Markets fluctuate between growth and contraction. Expansion periods are followed by corrections. Attempts to force constant growth often lead to instability. Sustainable systems account for cycles. Ignoring downturns does not prevent them. Preparing for them creates resilience.

Relationships thrive on balance between independence and intimacy. Too much autonomy creates distance. Excessive dependence suffocates. Healthy partnerships allow space and connection. Emotional availability coexists with personal boundaries. Polarity here does not divide partners. It creates structure.

Health statistics reinforce the need for balance. Chronic stress without recovery increases risk of cardiovascular disease. Sleep deprivation impairs cognitive function. Excessive caloric intake without physical activity leads to metabolic disorders. Extremes harm. Moderation protects. The body operates best within balanced ranges.

Spiritual maturity mirrors this physical pattern. Attempting to suppress every negative thought creates internal tension. Indulging every impulse leads to chaos. Discipline requires awareness of desire without surrendering to it. Compassion involves understanding anger without acting destructively upon it. Choosing the higher path does not mean pretending lower impulses never surface. It means guiding them.

Light for part of the day and darkness for the other half serves as a daily reminder that balance is not only natural but necessary. Every sunrise exists because a sunset came before it, and every period of rest is only possible after effort has been expended. The rhythm of the day quietly invites reflection without forcing it. Evening arrives and gives us a moment to pause, to look back at what we did well and what we might do differently next time. Morning arrives and opens a new door, offering another chance to choose direction with greater awareness. When you look closely, the pattern becomes obvious. If the natural world requires both light and dark in order to function, and if the human body depends on cycles of activity and recovery to stay healthy, then it makes little sense to expect the human mind or spirit to exist in constant light. Darkness, in some form, is part of the design.

Accepting this truth does not mean celebrating destructive behavior or allowing harmful impulses to control us. Instead, it means learning to understand the darker aspects of ourselves without immediately condemning them. Every person carries thoughts, emotions, and instincts that feel uncomfortable to admit, yet those parts of the psyche often exist for a reason. Fear can alert us to danger. Anger can rise when something unjust is happening. A strong protective instinct can appear when someone we love is threatened. There are moments in life when the shadow side of our nature rises not to destroy but to defend, to protect ourselves or the people who depend on us. The real problem begins when individuals stop guiding that energy and allow it to take control of their decisions. Darkness itself is not the enemy. Losing awareness of it is what leads people into destructive patterns.

For many people, a great deal of unnecessary suffering comes from believing that having dark thoughts makes them a bad person. Guilt forms, shame builds, and individuals begin fighting against parts of their own minds that were never meant to be completely erased. Let today be the moment you stop condemning yourself simply for having these thoughts and start looking at them differently. Instead of seeing darkness as proof of failure, recognize it as information. It reveals where you feel hurt, where you feel threatened, where you feel vulnerable, and where your values are strongest. Every difficult thought carries a lesson if you are willing to look at it honestly rather than bury it. When understood properly, those moments become opportunities for growth rather than sources of shame.

Understanding light becomes impossible without first experiencing darkness. The two are inseparable because comparison is what gives meaning to both. A person who has never faced hardship cannot truly appreciate peace and prosperity. Someone who has never felt loneliness may struggle to recognize the value of companionship. Joy becomes far more meaningful after pain has been experienced because it provides a reference point that gives gratitude depth. Without the contrast, emotions flatten into something dull and unremarkable. Darkness sharpens your awareness of light in the same way night makes the morning sun feel warmer and more welcoming. The contrast does not diminish the beauty of the light. It intensifies it.

The structure of the natural world reflects this same principle repeatedly. Oceans possess enormous power, yet they remain contained within the boundaries of their shorelines. Rivers move with tremendous force, but their direction is guided by the banks that hold them in place. Freedom exists within structure rather than in the absence of it.

The same concept applies to human beings. We are given the ability to choose, to think, and to act freely, yet our choices unfold within moral boundaries that exist for the stability of society and the protection of life itself. Rules and structure do not eliminate liberty. They guide it so that the power we possess does not destroy the very systems that sustain us.

When viewed this way, the presence of darkness in human nature stops looking like a flaw and begins to look more like an element of balance that requires awareness and responsibility. The goal is not to pretend the shadow does not exist, nor is it to allow it to dominate the mind unchecked. The real task is learning to recognize it, understand what it is trying to communicate, and direct that energy in ways that serve growth instead of destruction. Once a person learns to do that, the light within them becomes stronger, not weaker, because it is no longer fragile. It has been tested against darkness and chosen consciously.

Ignoring polarity leads to imbalance in our lives. Pretending only light exists creates fragility or weakness. Believing darkness defines everything produces despair and a mindset of doom only. Wholeness comes from recognizing both and aligning with what elevates your life.

Statistical data on habit formation underscores and emphasizes this truth. Research suggests that repeated behaviors strengthen neural pathways. Small daily choices compound over time become positive habits. Positive routines improve our mental health. Negative habits reinforce anxiety and depression. You consistent direction matters more than occasional deviation. If you find yourself veering off track, remember that you can always bring yourself back to center and re-route you behavior and you thinking pattern.

Polarity within human nature is not a curse. It is the framework that makes transformation possible. Growth requires this contrast. Courage develops in the presence of fear. Patience emerges in the presence of frustration. Generosity becomes meaningful where selfishness is an option. Being kind to yourself and another makes you feel good about yourself when you are aware of the opposite choice you could of made.

Creation reflects intentional balance. Light in everything serves purpose. Darkness also serves purpose. Human beings reflect that divine design. The responsibility lies in conscious alignment and choice. Every day offers the opportunity to participate in the design thoughtfully rather than re-actively. We were given the gift to choose how we show up in the world.

Polarity is not an enemy to defeat. It is a structure that helps us understand. Understanding leads to wiser choices and those choices shape our character. Our character shapes destiny.

Recognizing this design changes the conversation from shame to self management. Darkness within you does not demand condemnation. The goal is not for you to feel bad it is for you to grow and learn. It demands self mastery. Light within you does not guarantee perfection. It is a process that requires cultivation. The world operates through structured duality. Humanity operates exactly the same way.

The sun sets so that rest can occur. It rises so that activity can resume. Both phases are necessary. Human nature contains impulse and restraint, desire and discipline, self interest and compassion. Which side becomes dominant depends on repeated direction.

Polarity is everywhere and in everything. The evidence is visible in science, biology, psychology, and spirituality. Denying it does not dissolve it. Embracing awareness of it allows for intentional living.

Creation is not chaotic. It is patterned. Recognizing that pattern empowers you to move within it consciously. Each day places you between poles. Direction remains your responsibility.

#In59Seconds
EXPANSION
CONTRACTION

6

The Daily Return to Light

Every morning offers something far more powerful than scenery. It offers a opportunity to reset. When the sun rises, it does not argue with the night that came before it. It simply takes its place. Darkness does not resist. It yields to the beautiful sun. That quiet exchange happens every single day without drama or confrontation, there is no negotiation, and it does not fail. Light and dark understand their roles. Watching that rhythm teaches us something about how we are meant to live. We rise in the morning and rest at night. God designed that divine rhythm for a reason.

When I was a little girl growing up in Compton, California, there was a flower in our yard called the "Four O'Clock." Every single day, almost like it had an internal alarm set by God Himself, that flower would close up right at four in the afternoon. Its petals would fold in, and it would look as if it had withered away. Then morning would come, and without any dramatic announcement, it would be open again. Bright, alive and fully restored. As a child, I never stopped to think about what that meant. It was just something the flower did. Now, as a grown woman who understands seasons and the cycles of life, I am amazed by it. That flower was modeling something profound about life long before I had the language to describe it.

There are days when we close up, too. There are afternoons in life when disappointment, stress, betrayal, or exhaustion cause us to fold inward. We do not feel bright or open. We feel withdrawn and guarded. Maybe even a little wilted. In those moments, it can feel permanent, as if the heaviness will define us from that point forward. Yet the morning still comes. The sun still rises whether we feel ready for it or not. That natural reset carries a message that is easy to overlook: closure is not death, and darkness is not destiny. The fact that something closed yesterday does not mean it cannot open again today.

The beginning of each day represents choice in its purest form. Before you speak to anyone, before you scroll through messages, before the outside world starts making demands on your attention, there is a quiet internal moment where direction begins to form. Some mornings you wake up with weight on your chest, still carrying fragments of yesterday's frustration. Other mornings feel lighter, filled with gratitude or anticipation. Neither emotional state has the authority to dictate the entire day unless you surrender to it without awareness. What ultimately shapes the hours ahead is the decision you make once you recognize how you feel. The rising sun does not erase what happened yesterday, but it refuses to let yesterday have the final word.

Nature never rushes its transitions. Light does not crash violently into the sky at dawn; it slowly pushes back the dark until you suddenly realize the night has passed. That steady progression mirrors the way growth unfolds inside of us. Emotional maturity does not arrive in a single breakthrough moment.

Anger softens into patience gradually when you choose restraint repeatedly. Hurt transforms into understanding when you examine it honestly instead of feeding it resentment. Judgment loosens its grip when compassion is practiced on purpose. None of that happens instantly, and it is not supposed to. Balance is cultivated over time through countless small decisions that lean toward the higher side of who you are becoming.

The world itself demonstrates this rhythm daily. Seasons change without panic. Trees shed leaves without assuming they will never bloom again. Even the tide pulls back before it returns. Everything in creation models steady transition rather than abrupt transformation. The lesson is subtle but powerful: you do not have to become perfectly balanced overnight. You simply have to keep choosing to reopen. Keep choosing to lean toward light when you become aware that you are folding into shadow. Just like that Four O'Clock flower, you may close for a time, but you are designed to rise again.

When you choose the higher path in your own life, you begin to see more clearly where your habits need adjustment. Awareness can feel uncomfortable at first, but it is necessary for growth. You cannot change what you refuse to see.

As the day unfolds, opportunities for alignment appear constantly. Someone cuts you off in traffic. A coworker speaks sharply. A family member disappoints or disrespects you. Each moment becomes a fork in the road. You can respond from irritation or from intention. You can escalate the situation and make it worse or you can stabilize it. The world does not remove friction simply because you desire peace. The real practice of balance begins when friction shows up and you still choose the higher path.

Planning your emotional response deserves just as much

attention as planning your calendar. Most of us will map out meetings, appointments, and deadlines with precision, yet we walk into stressful environments without giving a single thought to how we intend to manage our reactions. A demanding boss with a harsh tone or a coworker who constantly interrupts can quietly pull you toward irritation before you even realize it. Long hours and mental fatigue chip away at patience, and when you are tired your self-control does not feel as strong as it does in the morning. Pressure has a way of exposing old patterns that you thought you had outgrown. Recognizing that rhythm ahead of time allows you to prepare for it instead of being blindsided by it. You can decide before the day even begins that no matter how chaotic it becomes, you will not let it drag you to the lower side of yourself. Holding a picture in your mind of the peaceful evening waiting for you at home can anchor you through the tension, reminding you that the workday is temporary but your character is constant.

As evening approaches, another quiet shift takes place. The light softens, the pace of the world slows, and your body begins to wind down. That transition creates space for you to reflect. Instead of replaying the day with harsh criticism, it helps to review it with honesty and compassion. There may have been moments when you responded better than you would have in the past, and there may have been moments when you slipped back into impatience. Growth is found in noticing both without tearing yourself apart. Accountability builds strength because it allows you to see where adjustment is needed. Self-condemnation, on the other hand, drains energy and erodes confidence. There is a clear difference between acknowledging that you lost your temper and telling yourself that you are a terrible person. One approach invites improvement, while the other keeps you stuck in shame.

Talking to yourself kindly after a difficult day does not mean you avoid responsibility. It means you understand that change happens through awareness, not abuse. When you look at your reactions with curiosity instead of judgment, you give yourself the opportunity to do better tomorrow. Each moment is an opportunity to return to light. Return to the person that you choose to be.

Each night becomes a chance to reset rather than relive your mistakes. That steady rhythm of preparation in the morning and reflection in the evening strengthens emotional balance over time. It turns ordinary workdays into training grounds for self-mastery, and it reminds you that even in environments you cannot control, you still have authority over the way you show up.

The setting sun reminds you that nothing is permanent, not even your mistakes. Light will always return. Another opportunity will present itself. Choosing the higher path is not about flawless performance. It is about consistent direction. Each day offers countless small chances to lean toward patience instead of anger, generosity instead of selfishness, calm instead of chaos.

Light and darkness are not enemies fighting for control of the sky. They are phases within a divine design. Human nature follows that same structure. Moments of frustration always will come. Moments of clarity will follow. The goal is not to eliminate the darker impulses completely. The goal is to manage them consciously and allow the light within you to lead more often than the shadows.

Daily life becomes sacred when you recognize this rhythm. Morning offers renewal. Afternoon demands discipline.

Evening invites reflection and the Night promises rest and restoration. The cycle repeats, not to trap you, but to train you. Every sunrise whispers the same truth: direction is always available.

7

What the Night Teaches

Night carries a different kind of power. It does not command attention the way daylight does. It invites stillness. When activity slows and distractions fade, the mind has space to surface what was ignored during the day. Some people fear that quiet because unresolved emotions tend to rise when noise disappears. Darkness has a way of revealing what busyness hides.

Polarity becomes deeply personal after sunset. Without the external demands of work and conversation, you are left alone with your thoughts. This is where many people confront the internal tug between higher intention and lower impulse. Regret may surface. Anxiety may attempt to replay the day. The mind can drift toward self criticism. Recognizing that this internal movement is natural prevents panic.

Rest requires trust. When you close your eyes at night, you surrender control temporarily. The body continues functioning without your supervision. The heart beats. The lungs breathe. Cells repair. That automatic restoration reflects divine design.

Effort governs the day. Renewal governs the night. Both are necessary. Continuous striving exhausts the soul. Continuous withdrawal weakens resilience. Balance lives in alternation.

The moon does not generate its own light. It reflects light from the sun. That reflection offers another lesson. During seasons when you feel dim, when your energy feels low, borrowed strength still counts. Encouragement from a friend, wisdom from a book, prayer, or memory of past victories can sustain you until your own brightness returns fully. Reflection is not weakness. It is partnership with something greater.

Night also clarifies scale. Looking up at the stars places daily frustrations in perspective. Problems that felt overwhelming at noon often shrink by midnight. The vastness of the sky humbles ego. It reminds you that your role in the world is meaningful but not absolute. Releasing the illusion of total control reduces internal tension.

Many breakthroughs occur during quiet hours. Insight often arrives when the mind stops racing. Solutions form when pressure eases. Emotional integration happens when you allow yourself to sit honestly with what you feel. Avoiding that process prolongs imbalance. Facing it gently promotes healing.

Transition from night back to morning represents one of the most powerful demonstrations of continuity. Darkness never defeats light permanently. Light never erases darkness permanently. The design cycles intentionally. Human growth follows the same rhythm. Periods of doubt do not mean you have failed. Periods of clarity do not mean you are finished evolving.

Choosing the higher path includes how you handle your evenings. Do you replay offenses and deepen resentment, or do you release them before sleep? Do you fuel anxiety with catastrophic thinking, or do you consciously redirect your focus? The internal decisions made in darkness often shape the tone of the following day.

Polarity within you does not disappear when the sun sets. It simply becomes quieter and more intimate. Night is not a threat. It is a teacher. It shows you what still needs attention. It offers rest where effort dominated. It prepares you to rise again with greater awareness.

Living consciously means honoring both phases. Act with integrity during the day. Reflect with honesty at night. Reset when morning comes. The design of creation provides the template. Your responsibility is participation.

#In59Seconds

8

Our Daily Choice

In Matthew 6:11, "Give us this day our daily bread" refers to nourishment for the body. Bread sustains physical life. Without it, the body weakens. What many people overlook is that the mind also requires daily nourishment. Just as food feeds the body, thoughts feed character. Each day we consume ideas, interpretations, reactions, and beliefs. Those mental choices either strengthen our higher nature or feed the lower impulses that exist within all of us. When viewed through the lens of polarity, daily bread becomes more than physical sustenance. It becomes the small, repeated choices we make that determine whether we move toward light or drift toward shadow.

Human beings do not wake up as blank slates. We wake up in the middle of polarity. Within us lives patience and irritation, generosity and selfishness, discipline and laziness, compassion and indifference. Those tendencies are not proof that we are flawed beyond repair. They are evidence that we were created with free will. The direction we take is rarely decided in dramatic, life-altering moments. It is decided in ordinary situations that appear insignificant. Those daily choices accumulate quietly, shaping identity, relationships, and destiny over time.

Major crises are obvious. Divorce, illness, betrayal, financial collapse, public humiliation. Anyone can identify those as defining moments. What often goes unnoticed are the smaller irritations that slowly train us toward bitterness or toward growth. A late client. A disrespectful tone. A forgotten holiday. A careless comment. A perceived rejection. These moments are where polarity becomes practical. They are opportunities to choose the higher path without applause, without witnesses, and often without anyone realizing that a battle even took place inside you.

Thought is the birthplace of direction. Before behavior appears, a narrative forms internally. A situation occurs, and the mind immediately interprets it. That interpretation creates emotion. Emotion influences response. Response shapes outcome. When people say they "lost control," what usually happened was that they accepted the first interpretation that surfaced and allowed it to drive them. Understanding polarity means recognizing that an initial thought is not a command. It is a suggestion. You still have authority.

Many fears are manufactured internally long before reality confirms them. Fear of failure, fear of abandonment, fear of being disrespected, fear of being overlooked. These experiences often begin as private conversations inside the mind. Rarely does someone stand in front of you and declare the worst things you believe about yourself. More often, those statements are whispered internally. If the mind repeatedly rehearses stories of rejection or inadequacy, emotional suffering becomes self-generated. That suffering feels real because the body responds to imagined threat almost the same way it responds to actual danger.

Learning to monitor thought is not about denying difficulty. It is about deciding which interpretation will govern your reaction. Polarity does not demand perfection. It demands awareness. The higher path is rarely the automatic one. It requires interruption of impulse. It requires questioning the story that forms instantly in the mind. It requires humility to admit that the first reaction may not be the wisest one.

Consider a situation that seems small. A loyal client arrives late and is short on payment. Irritation surfaces immediately. The mind begins constructing a case: he knew the rules, he had time to prepare, this shows disrespect. Anger feels justified. Remaining angry for four hours, however, is a choice. The loss of twenty dollars is measurable. The loss of peace is far more expensive. Remaining in resentment harms the person carrying it more than the person who caused it.

In that moment, polarity becomes visible. One direction leads toward bitterness, internal tension, and a lowered emotional state. The other direction requires gratitude, perspective, and restraint. Gratitude remembers years of loyalty. Perspective recognizes overall financial blessing. Restraint prevents an atmosphere of hostility from forming. The external outcome may be the same either way, but the internal state is drastically different. Choosing peace in a minor financial irritation strengthens the muscle needed for larger tests later.

The same principle applies within family relationships. A daughter offers to complete chores in exchange for money. Instructions are given, and the money is handed over prematurely. The chore is not completed thoroughly. Frustration rises. The mind immediately labels the behavior as ungrateful or entitled. The body tightens. Tone changes. Peace in the home shifts. Yet deeper reflection reveals that responsibility was shared. Money was given before the task was finished. The irritation partly belongs to the one who ignored her own inner warning.

Polarity in parenting is subtle. A harsh response may teach discipline, but it may also teach fear. A calm correction still communicates expectation without creating emotional damage. The intention may be good, but delivery determines whether light or shadow dominates the exchange. Choosing accountability over blame diffuses unnecessary suffering. That internal shift preserves harmony and models emotional maturity.

Small incidents throughout the day often hold more influence than dramatic ones because they repeat frequently. A friend fails to respond to a compliment. The mind concludes she is rude or dismissive. Another interpretation exists. Perhaps she struggles with self-worth and does not believe she deserves praise. Recognizing that possibility changes the emotional reaction immediately. Compassion replaces offense. Instead of withdrawing encouragement, one continues offering it without expectation of validation.

This is how understanding polarity transforms relationships. People operate from wounds that are not always visible. Dismissing them as unkind or arrogant may ignore deeper insecurity. Choosing a higher interpretation does not excuse harmful behavior, but it prevents unnecessary judgment when harm was never intended.

Emotional suffering is often self-generated through assumptions. A neighbor places an object inconveniently close to a driveway. Rather than initiating a respectful conversation, the mind builds a narrative of intentional disrespect. Each day that narrative grows stronger, even though no evidence supports it. Resentment accumulates over something that could be resolved with one calm request. Eventually the issue is addressed politely, and the neighbor responds kindly. Weeks of internal agitation could have been avoided by earlier communication.

This pattern repeats in countless forms. A store manager responds briefly and seems dismissive. The mind interprets it as rejection or ingratitude after a large purchase. Feelings are hurt. A tip is mentally withdrawn. Two blocks are walked in silent resentment. Later reflection reveals that no insult occurred. The reaction was fueled by personal sensitivity rather than actual offense. Emotional pain was self-created through interpretation.

Recognizing these patterns is essential in balancing good and evil within. Evil, in this context, is not monstrous cruelty. It is the small decision to nurture resentment instead of understanding, ego instead of humility, reaction instead of reflection. Good is the conscious choice to correct interpretation, extend grace, or take responsibility where appropriate.

Children provide another example of how polarity operates in subtle ways. A parent organizes an elaborate celebration filled with love and generosity. When the children forget to reciprocate on a smaller occasion, the initial reaction may be hurt. Thoughts arise questioning appreciation or importance. Yet the children quickly attempt to correct their oversight once they realize it. Choosing to feel wounded rather than understanding youthful forgetfulness would deepen unnecessary division.

Human beings crave appreciation. That desire is natural. Allowing it to morph into silent resentment when expectations are not immediately met is a choice. Recognizing love in the overall relationship prevents a single oversight from distorting perception. The higher path protects connection instead of feeding pride.

Romantic disappointment, job loss, financial strain, and relational conflict all present larger arenas for polarity. Immediate emotions may include anger, fear, or grief. Those emotions are human and valid. Remaining there indefinitely transforms pain into identity. Choosing to extract lessons, adjust strategy, and move forward reflects alignment with growth rather than stagnation.

Mental discipline does not eliminate hardship. It determines how hardship is processed. When anger becomes the primary lens through which life is viewed, decisions grow impulsive. When reflection interrupts anger, clarity returns. Clarity reduces damage. In many situations, a pause prevents words that cannot be taken back. A single harsh response can fracture trust built over years.

Anger feels powerful in the moment. It creates an illusion of control. Yet uncontrolled anger often hands control to the very circumstances it seeks to dominate. Choosing restraint protects dignity. Choosing compassion protects relationships. Choosing humility protects growth.

Polarity exists in every conversation. A disagreement can escalate into character attacks or evolve into mutual understanding. A mistake can become a source of shame or a catalyst for maturity. A slight inconvenience can become evidence of persecution or simply an ordinary part of life.

Each day provides countless micro-choices. Hold the door or let it close. Offer encouragement or remain silent. Speak respectfully or use sarcasm. Assume the best or assume the worst. None of these moments make headlines, yet collectively they define character.

Balancing good and evil is not about eliminating the shadow. It is about governing it. Irritation will arise. Pride will surface. Jealousy will appear. The presence of these emotions does not define you. What defines you is whether you feed them or redirect them. Emotional maturity involves acknowledging impulse without surrendering authority to it.

The mind is powerful. Every object in existence began as an idea. Every conflict began as a thought accepted without challenge. Every reconciliation began as a decision to move toward understanding instead of remaining in offense. Controlling thought patterns is not about toxic positivity. It is about moral clarity.

When insulted, you can retaliate or disengage. When disappointed, you can spiral into hopelessness or search for alternative paths. When criticized, you can harden defensively or evaluate whether growth is needed. These choices accumulate. Over time they shape temperament and reputation.

Choosing the higher path does not mean becoming passive or allowing abuse. Boundaries are essential. Respecting yourself is essential. Walking away from harmful dynamics is often necessary. The difference lies in whether separation is fueled by wisdom or revenge. You can distance yourself without hatred consuming your heart.

Daily bread, in this context, becomes daily discipline. It is the steady nourishment of integrity, patience, and self-examination. It is the consistent refusal to let fleeting irritation become permanent bitterness. It is the practice of pausing before responding. It is the decision to interpret situations through a lens of growth rather than grievance.

There will be moments when you fail. Everyone does. Words will be spoken too sharply. Assumptions will be made too quickly. Ego will occasionally win. Failure in a moment does not require surrendering the journey. Reflection allows correction. Correction strengthens awareness.

Growth occurs not through dramatic declarations but through repeated small victories. Each time resentment is replaced with gratitude, character strengthens. Each time ego yields to humility, wisdom increases. Each time anger is processed instead of unleashed, the higher path becomes more familiar.

Balancing good and evil within is a lifelong practice. No human reaches a permanent state of moral perfection. The objective is not flawless behavior. The objective is consistent direction. When mistakes occur, return to center. When pride rises, choose humility. When fear dominates, choose courage. When offense tempts retaliation, choose restraint.

The world improves when individuals improve. Societal harmony begins with private decisions. Every peaceful household began with someone deciding not to escalate tension. Every healed relationship began with someone choosing accountability over blame. Every transformed life began with a shift in thought.

Daily bread feeds the body. Daily discipline feeds the soul. Each morning you awaken in the middle of polarity. Each evening reflects the direction you chose. The higher path is rarely effortless, but it is always available. Choosing it consistently transforms not only your internal world but every environment you enter.

That is how we balance good and evil. Not through denial of shadow, but through daily governance of it. Not through grand gestures alone, but through steady correction in ordinary moments. Each thought is a seed. Each reaction is cultivation. Over time, the harvest reflects the choices made when no one else was watching.

9

Compassion in a World of Polarity

Understanding polarity within yourself changes the way you see other people. Once you accept that light and shadow both exist in your own nature, it becomes harder to sit comfortably on a pedestal of judgment. Awareness creates humility. Humility creates space for compassion. That compassion does not excuse harmful behavior, and it does not require you to tolerate abuse. It simply shifts the posture of your heart.

Most of us have witnessed someone operating from what we would call their darker side. Maybe it shows up as anger, manipulation, dishonesty, addiction, cruelty, or selfishness. The instinctive reaction is often rejection. We label quickly. We distance ourselves emotionally. We decide who they are based on what they did in that moment. What gets overlooked is the fact that human beings are not frozen in one expression. People operate from different parts of themselves at different times. You have done it. I have done it. The difference between someone who acts from love and someone who acts from fear often comes down to awareness and healing, not inherent worth.

It is convenient to forget who we used to be. Growth has a way of polishing our memory. Once you become more stable, more disciplined, more spiritually grounded, it becomes tempting to view others who are still struggling as inferior. Judgment feels powerful. It creates distance between you and the behavior you no longer want to identify with. That distance can protect your ego, but it can also harden your heart.

Recognizing polarity in human nature reminds you that everyone is capable of both generosity and selfishness, patience and impatience, honesty and deception. The difference is not that one person possesses darkness and another does not. The difference is which side they are currently feeding and whether they are conscious of their choice. Some people are still unconscious. Some are wounded. Some are repeating patterns they never examined. That does not make their behavior acceptable. It does make their humanity undeniable.

Compassion does not mean allowing someone to mistreat you. It does not mean staying in abusive environments. Boundaries are necessary. Distance is sometimes wise. Protection of your peace is non negotiable. The distinction lies in the internal posture you maintain. You can walk away without hatred. You can say no without contempt. You can refuse access without wishing destruction upon someone else. Compassion exists inside your heart even when separation exists in your actions.

When you truly understand polarity, you stop being shocked by human imperfection. Disappointment still happens, but surprise fades. Expecting flawless behavior from flawed people sets you up for constant resentment. Recognizing that everyone carries unresolved struggles fosters realistic expectations. That realism reduces unnecessary outrage.

Studies in psychology show that empathy increases when individuals are reminded of their own past mistakes. Research on moral humility suggests that people who reflect on times when they acted poorly become less punitive toward others. Memory softens judgment. Awareness expands understanding. This does not remove accountability. It balances it.

Communities thrive when compassion outweighs condemnation. Social science data consistently demonstrates that individuals with strong support systems are less likely to engage in destructive behavior. Isolation intensifies despair. Shame fuels secrecy. People who feel discarded often lean further into the very behaviors that caused rejection in the first place. That cycle does not justify harm, but it explains escalation.

Compassion interrupts that cycle. When someone is confronted firmly yet respectfully, the message carries weight without humiliation. When correction is delivered with dignity intact, growth becomes more likely. Harsh judgment often triggers defensiveness. Balanced accountability invites reflection.

Consider how you respond to your own failures. If every mistake resulted in self hatred, progress would stall. Internal growth requires the ability to acknowledge wrongdoing without destroying your sense of worth. The same principle applies outwardly. People change more effectively when they believe redemption is possible.

None of this denies the existence of extreme harm in the world. Violence, exploitation, and abuse are real. Legal consequences are necessary. Protective boundaries must be honored. Compassion does not cancel justice. Justice without compassion, however, can become vengeance. Balanced societies require both structure and mercy.

Polarity teaches that darkness often emerges from unaddressed pain. Trauma research reveals strong correlations between early childhood adversity and later aggressive or self destructive behaviors. Understanding that connection does not erase responsibility, but it expands context. Context fosters informed response rather than reactive condemnation.

When you observe someone acting from anger, ask yourself what fear might be underneath it. When you see dishonesty, consider what insecurity could be driving it. These questions do not excuse the behavior. They humanize the person behind it. Humanization prevents dehumanization. Dehumanization paves the way for cruelty.

Personal experience often provides the strongest lessons in compassion. Reflect on moments when you operated from your lower impulses. Perhaps you spoke harshly when stressed. Perhaps you withdrew when overwhelmed. Perhaps you made choices you regret deeply. During those seasons, what would have helped you more: humiliation or understanding combined with accountability? Most people heal faster in environments where correction is firm but not shaming.

Spiritual maturity involves seeing beyond the surface of behavior. It recognizes that identity is deeper than action. A person is not the sum total of their worst moment. Labeling someone permanently based on a single season ignores the dynamic nature of growth. Human beings evolve. Sometimes they regress. Sometimes they surprise you.

Compassion also protects your own internal state. Harboring resentment drains energy. Chronic anger affects blood pressure, sleep patterns, and overall well being. Studies link prolonged hostility to increased risk of cardiovascular disease. Carrying bitterness harms the carrier more than the target. Letting go benefits you physiologically as well as emotionally.

Balancing compassion with boundaries creates strength. Weakness tolerates abuse. Rigidity lacks empathy. Strength with empathy builds sustainable relationships. It allows you to say, "I will not accept this behavior, but I do not hate you." That sentence embodies polarity managed wisely.

Family systems often illustrate this balance clearly. Parents discipline children while still loving them. Consequences exist alongside care. Removal of privileges occurs within the context of belonging. Healthy correction communicates that behavior must change, not that identity is worthless.

The same principle applies in friendships and professional environments. You can address misconduct directly while maintaining respect. You can terminate employment without dehumanizing the individual. You can end a relationship without wishing suffering on the other person. Compassion shapes tone even when decisions are firm.

Recognizing polarity within yourself guards against hypocrisy. It keeps you aware that under different circumstances, you might have made similar choices. Gratitude for your own growth replaces arrogance. That humility softens your reactions to others.

A more compassionate society emerges when individuals internalize this awareness. Less public shaming. More constructive dialogue. Fewer immediate cancellations. More opportunities for repair. Social media often amplifies judgment. Outrage spreads faster than understanding. Choosing compassion becomes countercultural.

Supporting accountability structures while maintaining empathy reflects mature balance. Courts administer justice. Communities provide rehabilitation. Families offer guidance. Individuals cultivate forgiveness internally. Each level plays a role.

None function optimally when compassion disappears entirely.

Understanding duality also reduces self righteousness. Recognizing your capacity for both harm and healing prevents moral superiority. Growth becomes ongoing rather than complete. You remain vigilant about your own tendencies rather than obsessing over others'.

Compassion does not guarantee reciprocation. Some people will continue harmful patterns despite understanding. Maintaining your boundaries remains essential. Protecting your well being is not selfish. It is responsible stewardship of your life. Compassion exists internally even when access is restricted externally.

The goal of balancing good and what we call evil within human nature is not naïveté. It is clarity. Clarity sees behavior accurately without exaggeration. It refuses to ignore wrongdoing. It also refuses to strip away humanity.

When more people feel supported rather than discarded, cycles of harm decrease. Belonging reduces desperation. Connection reduces hostility. Empathy reduces isolation. The ripple effect of individual compassion extends further than most people realize.

Choosing compassion daily aligns with the higher path described throughout this book. Every encounter becomes an opportunity to practice it. You may not be able to transform everyone you meet. You can transform the way you respond.

A world with less condemnation and more accountability balanced with empathy would look different. Fewer people would feel like permanent outcasts. More would feel invited to evolve. Healing spreads when shame decreases.

Polarity ensures that darker impulses will continue to surface in humanity. Compassion ensures that light has a chance to guide the response. Holding both truths simultaneously strengthens your character and contributes to collective healing.

Each day you wake up positioned between judgment and understanding. Which direction you choose influences more than your personal peace. It shapes the emotional climate of every room you enter. Compassion is not weakness. It is disciplined strength informed by awareness of your own humanity.

#In59Seconds

10

Emotional Control Is a Choice

Polarity does not only live in philosophy or nature. It lives in your nervous system. It lives in the split second between what happens to you and how you respond. Emotional control is not about becoming robotic or pretending you do not feel anger, frustration, or fear. It is about deciding whether those emotions will drive your behavior or inform it. That distinction can change the entire direction of your life.

Reactive behavior is the most visible expression of unmanaged polarity. Something happens inside of you. A nerve is touched, your pride is bruised. Someone challenges your authority and disrespects you. Instead of pausing, the darker impulse within you surges forward and harsh words fly out. You actions begin to escalate and at time irreversible consequences follow. In that moment, the lower path feels powerful and satisfying. You feel justified in your reactive behavior. It makes you feel strong at the time but later, it often reveals itself as self sabotage and destructive behavior. We have all been there. Noticing the behavior is the first step in changing it.

Sometimes, to unwind, I watch police bodycam footage online. Those videos are sobering. A simple traffic stop turns into chaos because someone cannot regulate their emotions. A minor ticket becomes an arrest because pride overrides reason. People scream, curse, spit, resist, and fight officers over something that could have been handled calmly in five minutes. Watching it unfold is painful because the outcome is so unnecessary. Lives get altered over ego and impulse.

In many of those videos, you can see the exact moment where polarity presents itself. An officer approaches the car. The driver feels irritated. They are faced with a choice, to cooperate or be confrontational. They can breathe or explode, listen and comply or react. Some people choose to comply respectfully, handle the citation, and go home safely. Others allow anger to take control. The difference between those two outcomes is emotional regulation.

Emotional control can literally save your life. It can prevent physical harm. It can prevent legal trouble. It can prevent damaged relationships. It can prevent lost opportunities. The inability to manage reactive impulses has destroyed careers, marriages, friendships, and reputations. A few uncontrolled minutes can undo years of effort.

None of this suggests that people do not have valid reasons to feel upset. There are situations that are unfair. There are authorities who abuse power. There are moments when frustration is understandable. The issue is not whether the emotion is justified. The issue is whether the reaction will improve or worsen the situation.

Neuroscience explains part of this dynamic. When you perceive a threat, the amygdala activates quickly. The body releases stress hormones. Heart rate increases. Muscles tense. The fight or flight response prepares you for action. That response evolved to protect you from physical danger. In modern life, however, it activates in social and emotional situations that do not require physical combat. Without awareness, that surge can hijack rational thought.

The prefrontal cortex, which governs reasoning and impulse control, needs a moment to engage. That moment is small, sometimes only seconds. Emotional maturity develops in that space. Pausing allows logic to catch up with emotion. Failing to pause hands control over to instinct.

Polarity appears here again. Impulse and restraint exist side by side. The lower impulse demands immediate expression. The higher path invites consideration. Both are present. Which one you empower determines the outcome.

Reactive behavior can feel powerful in the moment. When someone offends you or challenges you, snapping back seems like strength. Raising your voice releases tension. Firing off a sharp response can create the illusion that you have regained control. There is a rush that comes with expressing indignation. For a few seconds, it feels satisfying. What it almost never does is fix the real problem. Most of the time it multiplies it.

Energy responds to energy. Escalation invites escalation. When you throw heat into a situation, the temperature rises. Very rarely does anger extinguish anger. What you project outward tends to come back amplified. That does not mean you are responsible for other people's behavior, but it does mean you influence the emotional climate around you more than you may realize.

Calm works the same way. When you slow your breathing, lower your tone, and refuse to match someone's aggression, something shifts. The room can feel it. The conversation often softens. Not every time, because some people are committed to chaos, but often enough that it is worth practicing. Composure does not make you weak. It makes you steady. Steadiness changes outcomes.

You are not obligated to mirror the energy that is thrown at you. Someone else's combative mood does not require your participation. Choosing not to return aggression with aggression is not submission. It is control. It is the quiet understanding that you do not have to join every fight you are invited to.

On May 30, 2024, my patience with dating was running thin. Instead of easing into conversation and allowing chemistry to unfold naturally, I reached a point where I wanted immediate clarity. After matching with a man named William E on Facebook Dating, I told him to meet me right away. I had no desire to spend days building emotional momentum only to discover we were incompatible. To my surprise, he agreed. We met in Florence at a place I frequent called Tals Café. He was tall, well groomed, and greeted me with a warm smile and an easygoing spirit. Breakfast flowed effortlessly. We shared stories about life, loss, and resilience. He spoke about the recent death of his mother and became emotional at the table. I comforted him and shared painful losses from my own life. That vulnerability created an immediate bond.

The relationship moved quickly into exclusivity, and for a while everything appeared ideal. He was attentive in ways many women dream about. Every door was opened. Every bill was paid. He was generous with my children and willing to participate in the social world I had created. He enjoyed being on camera and happily appeared in our Instagram and TikTok videos. He never declined an invitation and always seemed ready to accompany me anywhere. At first, that level of attentiveness felt flattering. Over time, some of it became excessive. Wiping my mouth after meals without asking or deciding when I was thirsty and lifting a glass to my lips crossed into territory that felt less like love and more like control disguised as care.

As the months passed, deeper concerns began to surface. He had no hobbies, no clear goals, no dreams he spoke about building. Conversations about his past were filled with negativity toward former wives, family members, and friends. He described severing relationships almost as a badge of honor. That pattern unsettled me. I introduced him to my positive outlook and he would agree in theory, yet there was no evidence of internal change. It felt as if he preferred performing the role of growth rather than committing to the work required for it.

By the fourth month, during a card party at my home with friends and children present, his shadow side emerged in a way that could no longer be ignored. In previous gatherings I had gently told him that his tone during games felt aggressive. He carried himself as the authority in the room, emphasizing his forty years of experience as though everyone else were incompetent. That dominant demeanor made others uncomfortable. On this particular night, because I was engaging with guests rather than centering him, he began spiraling. He stormed in and out of the house, demanded private conversations, and grew visibly agitated over trivial issues related to the card game. When I calmly declined to step outside again, he snatched a card box from the table and created a scene in front of everyone. His inability to regulate his emotions in a room full of witnesses made something very clear to me.

This is exactly where the theme of this book lives. 90% of the time he was a really nice and happy man. I am not labeling him evil. I am saying that in those moments he surrendered to the darker side of himself. His pride overrode his humility and his anger overrode composure. The choice he made in that heated moment cost him the entire relationship. Had he paused, breathed, and regulated his frustration and not behaved like a child, the evening could have unfolded differently. Emotional control is not about suppressing feelings. It is about choosing not to let those feelings drive destructive behavior.

The situation triggered deep childhood memories for me, especially witnessing violence in my early years. Despite the fear that surfaced, I chose calm. I refused to escalate. I stayed seated. I responded without hostility. That choice mattered. Emotional control as a choice became visible in real time. One of us allowed shadow to dominate. One of us chose restraint. The outcome followed accordingly.

Balancing good and evil in human nature does not mean eliminating anger or insecurity. It means recognizing when those emotions surface and deciding which side of yourself will lead. There are people sitting in prison cells because they surrendered to a two second impulse. There are marriages destroyed because pride refused to bend. There are friendships severed because someone chose retaliation over reflection. The battlefield is often internal long before it becomes external.

When I left that relationship, I did not leave with bitterness. I left with life lessons. I learned that generosity and charm do not replace character. I learned that attentiveness without self regulation can morph into control. I learned that love cannot thrive where emotional discipline is absent. Most importantly, I learned that my inability to develop deep feelings was not confusion. It was intuition recognizing instability beneath the surface.

Emotional control is one of the clearest demonstrations of how to balance good and evil within yourself. Anger can be felt without being weaponized. Fear can be acknowledged without being projected. Frustration can be expressed without humiliation. The shadow side of human nature is not proof that someone is doomed. It becomes destructive only when indulged without awareness. Choosing the higher side requires discipline, humility, and self observation.

That relationship became a living example of this book's message. Good and evil are not abstract forces floating in the universe. They show up in living rooms, at card tables, in romantic partnerships, and in ordinary disagreements. In every tense moment, there is a choice. The side you feed grows stronger. The side you restrain weakens. Learning to recognize that internal tug of war and deliberately choose composure over chaos is how we protect our peace and our future.

Watching those bodycam videos I spoke of earlier reinforces this lesson repeatedly. Some individuals sabotage themselves not because they are incapable of better choices, but because they refuse to manage the emotional surge in front of them. The tragedy lies in how preventable many of those outcomes are.

Polarity within you is neutral until activated. Every morning you wake up with the capacity to respond thoughtfully or react impulsively. Stressful situations will arise. Someone will offend you. Something will inconvenience you. That moment does not define you. Your response does.

Learning emotional control requires daily practice. It begins with awareness of your own triggers. Identify what sets you off quickly. be it disrespect, delays, feeling ignored, financial pressure. Once you recognize patterns, you can prepare for them. Preparation strengthens the discipline needed to change them.

Breathing techniques, mental reframing, and physical movement all support regulation. Slowing your breath signals safety to the nervous system. Reframing the situation reduces perceived threat. Stepping away momentarily prevents escalation. These tools may seem simple, but their impact is profound.

Accountability also plays a role. When you do react poorly, reflection matters. What triggered you? What belief fueled the reaction? How could you respond differently next time? Growth requires honest evaluation without self condemnation.

Emotional control also influences the energy you bring into shared spaces. One reactive individual can destabilize an entire room. One steady individual can calm it. Leadership, whether formal or informal, depends heavily on this ability.

The concept of balancing good and evil becomes practical here. Evil, in this context, does not refer to dramatic criminal acts alone. It includes small daily decisions to lash out, to humiliate, to intimidate, or to escalate unnecessarily. Good includes restraint, understanding, measured response, and thoughtful communication. The battlefield is ordinary life.

Parenting provides a powerful example. A child tests limits. The parent feels irritation rising. Reacting harshly may silence the child temporarily but damages trust. Responding firmly yet calmly teaches discipline without fear. The outcome differs drastically based on emotional control.

Relationships follow the same pattern. An argument begins. Old wounds surface. Words that cannot be taken back hover at the edge of the tongue. Choosing silence for a moment can prevent permanent damage. Many relationships end not because of disagreement, but because of uncontrolled reaction during disagreement.

Public spaces give you constant chances to practice this kind of discipline, whether you feel ready or not. Standing in a grocery store line while a cashier speaks to you with an edge in her voice can stir something up quickly. A driver cutting you off in traffic can make your heart race and your jaw tighten in seconds. A colleague brushing past your idea in a meeting as if you never spoke can feel like a personal attack. None of these moments are life-altering on their own, yet each one carries a subtle invitation. You can allow irritation to take over and respond in a way that adds more hostility to the environment, or you can steady yourself and choose a response that reflects who you are trying to become.

It is easy to justify snapping back when someone is rude. Part of you wants to teach them a lesson, to match their tone so they understand how it feels. In that split second, the darker side of your nature whispers that retaliation is strength. The higher side quietly reminds you that reacting in anger often creates more mess than resolution. Deciding to remain composed does not mean you are weak or passive. It means you understand that multiplying negativity rarely improves a situation. You are not responsible for their lack of patience or poor communication skills, but you are responsible for whether you allow their behavior to drag you into a version of yourself you do not respect.

Traffic is another powerful classroom. Someone speeds past you, honks aggressively, or rides your bumper as if your existence is an inconvenience. The impulse to speed up, glare, or return the aggression can feel automatic. Choosing to slow your breathing instead of escalating may prevent an accident or at the very least protect your own nervous system from unnecessary stress. Maintaining calm in those moments keeps your body from absorbing tension that does not belong to you. It allows you to arrive at your destination with your peace intact rather than carrying the residue of a stranger's impatience.

Work environments provide even more subtle tests. A dismissive comment from a coworker can echo in your mind for hours if you let it. You can replay the exchange repeatedly, crafting sharper responses you wish you had delivered. That mental rehearsal often prolongs the hurt and strengthens resentment. Taking a breath and deciding to address the issue thoughtfully later, or even to let it go entirely if it is not worth the energy, keeps you from building a narrative that damages your mood for the rest of the day. Emotional maturity sometimes looks like choosing which battles deserve your voice and which ones deserve your silence.

Every one of these interactions may seem small, yet they accumulate. The way you handle the minor irritations shapes how you will handle the major crises. Balancing good and bad within yourself is not reserved for dramatic moments; it is practiced in grocery stores, on highways, in offices, and in living rooms. Each time your feelings are hurt, you are given an opportunity to decide whether you will act from wounded pride or from grounded self-awareness. The more often you choose the higher response, the more natural it becomes. Over time, that discipline forms character, and character determines the overall direction of your life.

Emotional control does not excuse anyone else's behavior, and it does not mean you pretend that hurtful actions are acceptable. People are responsible for what they say and what they do. If someone lies, disrespects you, manipulates you, or behaves in a cruel way, that accountability belongs to them. Learning to govern your own emotions does not shift their responsibility onto your shoulders. What it does is give you ownership over yourself. It gives you the power to decide how you will respond instead of allowing someone else's chaos to dictate your character. That kind of ownership is deeply empowering because it means your behavior is no longer dependent on theirs. It reflects growth. It moves your attention away from constant blame and toward internal discipline, which is the only part of any situation you truly control.

When you realize that your peace is not at the mercy of another person's mood, something changes inside of you. Instead of obsessing over what they should have done differently, you begin asking yourself how you want to show up. That shift is quiet but profound. It transforms you from someone reacting to life into someone directing your own conduct within it. This does not mean you tolerate disrespect or stay in unhealthy situations. It means that even when you have to walk away, you do so with composure instead of collapse. Emotional discipline allows you to leave a room, end a relationship, or set a boundary without destroying your own integrity in the process.

There is also a deeper spiritual layer to this kind of self-regulation. Across cultures and traditions, self-mastery has always been considered a sign of maturity. The ability to restrain the tongue when harsh words are tempting, to steady your temper when anger surges, and to practice patience when frustration feels justified are not small accomplishments. They reflect alignment with the higher aspect of human nature. They show that you are not driven solely by impulse but guided by intention. That alignment is strength. It requires awareness, humility, and practice. It asks you to rise above instinct and choose character.

Strength is often misunderstood as loudness or dominance, but true strength is the capacity to hold yourself together when everything around you feels unstable. It is the decision to remain thoughtful when provoked. It is the refusal to let a temporary emotion produce a permanent consequence. Self-mastery is not weakness disguised as politeness. It is power exercised with restraint. When you learn to govern yourself, you begin to embody the higher side of who you are meant to be, and that embodiment influences every relationship and environment you step into.

No one wakes up one day and masters emotional control completely. That is not how this works. There will be moments when you react too quickly, speak too sharply, or let your feelings get ahead of your wisdom. That does not mean you have failed as a person. It means you are human. The point is not to perform perfectly. The point is to become more aware and a little better than you were yesterday. Every time you pause instead of exploding, every time you choose to lower your voice instead of raising it, you are strengthening something inside of you. You are building the muscle of restraint. Over time, those pauses become more natural. Your identity slowly shifts into someone who responds thoughtfully rather than reacts impulsively.

When I watch those bodycam videos I mentioned earlier, where people lose control over something as small as a traffic stop, I do not watch them with judgment. I watch them with awareness. You can literally see the moment where the situation could have gone one way or the other. One choice, one breath, one sentence spoken differently could have changed everything. Instead, pride kicks in, anger takes over, and within seconds someone is in handcuffs or worse. Those moments follow people for years. They affect jobs, families, reputations, and futures. Emotional control in that instant could have created an entirely different outcome. That is how powerful self-regulation really is.

Balancing what we call good and evil inside yourself is not about pretending you never feel rage, jealousy, or resentment. It is about recognizing those feelings without letting them drive the car. The darker impulses that rise up in you are not proof that you are corrupt or beyond hope. They are reminders that you have power. They are invitations to practice discipline. When you consistently choose the higher response, even when it is hard, you build character that cannot be shaken easily. Over time, that discipline becomes part of who you are, and the version of you that once reacted without thinking begins to lose its grip..

Freedom is not the ability to do whatever you feel in the moment. Freedom is the ability to choose wisely despite what you feel. Emotional control anchors that freedom. It protects your future from your temporary emotions.

Polarity guarantees that both reaction and restraint will always be options. Growth ensures that restraint becomes your default more often than reaction. The world does not need more explosive responses. It needs more steady individuals capable of pausing before acting.

Every day presents situations that test your regulation. Every day offers chances to practice mastery. Emotional control is not glamorous. It is powerful. It quietly determines whether your life moves toward stability or chaos.

Balancing good and evil begins internally. The choice between reactive behavior and thoughtful response is one of the clearest examples of that balance in action. Your life improves in direct proportion to your ability to govern yourself. That governance is not repression. It is wisdom in motion.

11

The Discipline of the Higher Path

Living between good and evil is not dramatic most of the time. It is not always about life and death decisions or massive moral crossroads. More often, it shows up in quiet, ordinary discipline. It is the discipline of choosing who you want to be when no one is applauding you, when no one is correcting you, and when you could easily get away with less than your best.

The higher path is rarely the easiest path. It asks for restraint when you want revenge. It asks for honesty when lying would be simpler. It asks for humility when pride is screaming to defend itself. That tension is not a flaw in your character. It is the design of polarity working itself out in real time. Within you lives the capacity to elevate a situation and the capacity to damage it. The difference is rarely talent. It is discipline.

Discipline is not punishment. It is self leadership. It is the ability to guide your own behavior according to your values rather than your impulses. People often admire strength in others without realizing how much quiet self control it requires. The person who walks away from gossip when everyone else is leaning in has exercised discipline. The individual who refuses to retaliate publicly, even when attacked, has chosen strength over ego.

In a world that rewards quick reactions and loud opinions, discipline can look boring. It does not trend online. It does not always receive immediate validation. What it does is build integrity. Integrity forms when your private behavior matches your public values. That alignment creates internal peace. Without it, success feels hollow.

Polarity reveals itself clearly in ambition as well. The drive to succeed can uplift or corrupt. You can pursue excellence while remaining ethical, or you can chase achievement at the expense of others. History is filled with brilliant individuals who allowed their darker impulses to override their gifts. Talent alone does not determine destiny. Character does.

Choosing the higher path sometimes means absorbing discomfort. It may require being misunderstood. It may involve letting someone think they won an argument you chose not to escalate. That restraint can feel unfair in the moment. Over time, it strengthens your reputation and your peace.

Emotional maturity plays a central role here. Discipline does not suppress emotion; it organizes it. You can feel deeply without acting recklessly. You can experience disappointment without becoming destructive. Self regulation creates space between feeling and behavior. That space is where growth happens.

The temptation to justify lower impulses often disguises itself as authenticity. People say they are simply being real when they unleash anger or sarcasm. Authenticity without wisdom becomes carelessness. Being genuine does not require being harmful. Strength does not require intimidation.

Polarity within human nature ensures that you will face moments when your darker side seems reasonable. You will hear internal arguments that support bitterness or retaliation. You will feel the pull toward shortcuts. Recognizing those thoughts without automatically agreeing with them is part of self mastery.

Spiritual development involves becoming aware of the voice inside that nudges you upward. Conscience speaks quietly. Ego tends to shout. The higher path rarely demands attention through force. It invites alignment. Listening requires intention.

Discipline also influences how you handle success. Power amplifies character. If humility is weak, authority can become abusive. If generosity is strong, influence can uplift others. Wealth, recognition, and leadership magnify whatever already exists internally. Preparing your character before those opportunities arrive protects you from misusing them.

Everyday interactions offer practice. When someone praises you, discipline prevents arrogance. When someone criticizes you unfairly, discipline prevents collapse or retaliation. When no one is watching, discipline governs integrity. These moments accumulate. They shape identity gradually.

Balancing good and evil is not about eliminating temptation. It is about strengthening your commitment to your chosen direction. Commitment grows through repetition. Each disciplined decision reinforces the identity you are building. Each uncontrolled reaction weakens it.

There will be days when you fall short. Discipline includes accountability. Owning mistakes without spiraling into shame demonstrates maturity. Correcting course quickly keeps you aligned with your values. Refusing to acknowledge error strengthens the lower impulses you are trying to manage.

Community influences discipline as well. Surrounding yourself with people who respect integrity reinforces your standards. Constant exposure to environments that normalize chaos weakens resolve. Choosing relationships wisely supports your higher path.

The discipline of the higher path also requires self compassion. Harsh self criticism often leads to discouragement rather than improvement. Growth thrives in environments where effort is recognized, even when perfection is absent. Encouraging yourself does not mean excusing yourself. It means believing in your capacity to evolve.

Polarity guarantees that discipline will remain necessary throughout your life. Advancement does not eliminate temptation. Aging does not remove ego. Success does not silence insecurity. Vigilance must remain active. Awareness keeps you grounded.

Living intentionally becomes easier with practice. Habits form. Patience strengthens. Reactivity decreases. Others begin to notice your steadiness. Influence expands quietly. Leadership becomes natural rather than forced.

The higher path is not glamorous. It is consistent. It shows up in daily routines, private conversations, financial decisions, and personal boundaries. It reveals itself in how you treat those who cannot benefit you and how you respond when no one is judging you.

Balancing good and evil within yourself requires accepting responsibility for your choices. External circumstances influence you, but they do not control you completely. Freedom exists in your response. Discipline protects that freedom.

The world benefits from individuals who choose steadiness

over chaos. Families feel safer. Workplaces become healthier. Communities grow stronger. Each disciplined choice contributes to a larger culture of accountability and compassion.

Living this way does not mean you will never feel the pull of your darker side. It means you refuse to let it lead. The higher path is not automatic. It is intentional. It is practiced. It is strengthened through repetition.

Every day you stand between impulse and integrity. The direction you choose shapes the person you become. Discipline is the bridge between who you are and who you intend to be. Walking that bridge consistently transforms polarity from a battlefield into a training ground.

12

Choosing the Higher Side of Yourself

Before you close this book, I want to say something clearly and without hesitation. Do not be offended by the word evil. Do not let that word push you away from this message or make you feel accused. This book was never written to label you, shame you, or place you in some dramatic category of good versus wicked. When I use that word, I am not talking about monsters hiding in the shadows. I am talking about the everyday pull toward selfishness, cruelty, bitterness, dishonesty, or indifference that lives in all of us if we are honest enough to admit it.

Evil, in the context of this book, is not about serial killers and headlines. It is about love or hate, kindness or cruelty, the quiet choice to gossip when you could stay silent. It is about the moment you know you are wrong but double down anyway. It is about choosing pride over peace. It is about allowing anger to take the wheel when patience would have protected everyone involved. If that definition feels more human and less horrifying, then you understand what I have been trying to say from the beginning.

Polarity is not something that exists outside of you. It lives within you everyday. You wake up each day positioned between two directions. You can move toward compassion or toward contempt. You can move toward discipline or toward impulse. You can move toward healing or toward harm. That movement does not require a dramatic event. It shows up in the smallest interactions.

This is not a book about fear. It is a book about awareness. The moment you recognize that you carry both light and shadow, you gain power. Power to choose. Power to pause. Power to redirect yourself before damage is done. That awareness does not condemn you. It equips you.

There is something deeply freeing about admitting that you are capable of falling short. It removes the exhausting pressure to appear perfect. It allows you to stop pretending that you are immune to darker impulses. Once you acknowledge them, you can manage them. What you deny will control you. What you face can be guided.

Understanding good and evil as daily choices rather than fixed identities changes everything. You are not permanently good because you had a kind moment, and you are not permanently evil because you had a cruel one. You are a human being navigating polarity. What defines you is the direction you consistently choose.

Some readers may still resist the language. The word evil can feel heavy because of how it has been used historically. It has been used to condemn, exclude, and divide. That is not the spirit in which it appears here. Here, it is a mirror. A reminder. A tool for self examination. If the word feels strong, let it be strong enough to wake you up, not strong enough to shame you.

You were created with freedom. Freedom is sacred because

it allows love to be real. Without the possibility of selfishness, generosity would mean nothing. Without the option to harm, kindness would not carry weight. The presence of polarity is not a design flaw. It is the framework that makes moral choice meaningful.

When you see someone operating from their lower impulses, remember that you have stood in that place before in some form. That memory should soften your judgment without weakening your boundaries. You can protect yourself and still wish growth for others. You can walk away and still hope they evolve. Compassion and caution can coexist.

The world improves one regulated reaction at a time. One honest conversation at a time. One disciplined decision at a time. Grand change begins with private alignment. If more people understood that their daily emotional choices contribute to the collective atmosphere, communities would feel different.

The higher path is not reserved for saints. It is available to ordinary people who decide to be conscious. It requires humility. It requires reflection. It requires courage to admit when you were wrong and strength to do better next time. None of those qualities are signs of weakness. They are evidence of growth.

There will be days when you choose poorly. There will be moments when your temper outruns your wisdom. There will be seasons when you drift further from your ideals than you would like. That does not disqualify you from choosing differently tomorrow. Redemption is built into the design of each new day.

Every sunrise presents the same quiet question. Which side of yourself will you empower today? The impatient side or the patient one. The bitter side or the forgiving one. The reactive side or the disciplined one. The answer is rarely dramatic. It is revealed in tone of voice, in posture, in the words you decide to speak or swallow.

Balancing good and evil is not about achieving some flawless moral state. It is about staying awake to your own influence. It is about refusing to let your darker impulses operate unconsciously. It is about remembering that your smallest choices ripple outward into families, workplaces, and communities.

You are not powerless in this design. You are not a victim of your emotions. You are not trapped by your past. Polarity may exist within you, but direction remains yours. That truth should not frighten you. It should strengthen you.

If you take nothing else from these pages, take this: the presence of a darker side does not make you broken. It makes you a human being. The consistent choice to rise above it makes you wise. Do not be offended by the word evil. Be awakened by it. Let it remind you that the higher path is always available, and that every day you are given the dignity of choosing it.

HIGHER YOU
LOWER YOU

About the Author

SaBrina Fisher Reece was once known throughout California as "The Braid Queen." For more than twenty-six years, she owned and operated the legendary Braids By SaBrina, a celebrated salon and school on Adams Boulevard in Los Angeles. It grew into the largest and most influential braiding establishment in the city, where artistry, empowerment, discipline, and community came together in powerful ways. Her success was entirely self-made, built through perseverance, resilience, and vision, often without consistent external support or validation.

As she stepped into the second half of her life, SaBrina felt a deeper calling unfolding within her. The story behind her success was not just one of entrepreneurship, but one of faith, healing, self-trust, and spiritual awakening. Early experiences of abandonment and profound personal loss led her inward, where she began the real work of emotional healing and inner mastery. What started as creative expression evolved into purposeful transformation.

Today, SaBrina writes self-help books rooted in emotional healing, personal growth, and spiritual awareness. Blending lived experience with motivational insight and metaphysical understanding, she explores themes of balance, resilience, self-mastery, and the unseen forces that shape human thought and behavior. Through her writing and motivational speaking, she guides readers toward deeper self-awareness, renewed confidence, and lives that feel intentional and aligned from the inside out.

She is the author of numerous self-help and transformational works, including *My Spiritual Smile*, *Kicking Depression In the Butt*, *Your Mind Is Magic*, *Perfectly Positive*, *Living Life on a Higher Frequency*, *Spiritual Balance*, *Angry World*, *Become Your Own Cheerleader*, God is Not a Man: Rediscovering the Divine Balance of Masculine and Feminine Within Us All, *Self Sabotage*, *How to Get Exactly What You Want From God*, *When I Say "I Am"*, and the popular Ebooks: *Imagine: Learn How to Use Your Imagination to Design the Life You Desire*, *You're Not Religious -You're Spiritual-I Get It: Bridging the Gap Between the Two*, , *Take A Breath With Bri: The Power of Intentional Breathing*, *Is This Why They Burned The Books?: Buried Wisdom From The Past.*

Her passion for sound and frequency has led her to explore the healing power of crystal sound bowls, tuning forks, and flow chimes, tools designed to help harmonize the body, mind, and spirit. Now residing in the enchanting landscapes of New Mexico, "The Land of Enchantment," she offers Sound Vibration Sessions that invite others to slow down, breathe deeply, and reconnect with their higher selves. While she embraces these modalities, she reminds her students and readers that there is no single path to peace. Every journey is sacred, and every sincere method of connecting with the Divine carries value.

Above all, SaBrina is a devoted mother of four, Justin, Joi, Jayden, and Journey, and a proud grandmother to Raiden Jesse and Rio Jordan. Watching them, and those she teaches, awaken to their divine potential remains her greatest joy.

Her message is simple and enduring: we are each born with divine energy, a God-given power to create, to heal, and to live fully. The goal is not perfection, but peace. The journey is not to escape life, but to embrace it, to use positive tools to take control of the mind and become the master of your fate.

You can connect with me on:

https://in59secondspublishing.com

https://www.facebook.com/BraidQueenSaBrinaReece

Also by SaBrina Fisher Reece

SaBrina Fisher Reece writes self-help books rooted in emotional healing, personal growth, and spiritual awareness. Her work blends lived experience with motivational insight, often exploring themes of balance, resilience, self-mastery, and the unseen forces that shape our thoughts and behaviors. Drawing from both practical reflection and metaphysical concepts, her writing encourages readers to develop greater self-awareness, reconnect with their inner strength, and create more intentional, aligned live

Kicking Depression in the Butt is a raw, faith-infused, and deeply practical guide for anyone who is tired of surviving in silence and ready to reclaim their life.

Drawing from her own lived experiences with trauma, abandonment, loss, and depression, SaBrina Fisher Reece invites readers into an honest conversation about what depression really feels like,and how to fight back. This book does not minimize pain or offer shallow positivity. Instead, it helps readers recognize depression as an internal enemy, interrupt destructive thought cycles, and rebuild their inner world with intention, truth, and daily tools that actually work.

Through personal storytelling, spiritual insight, and mindset-shifting strategies, SaBrina shows readers how to stop identifying with their darkest thoughts and begin designing a life that protects their peace. She addresses the realities of trauma, triggers, boundaries, faith, therapy, medication, and personal responsibility, offering a balanced approach that honors both professional support and inner work.

Kicking Depression in the Butt is for the person who keeps showing up while quietly falling apart. It is for those who smile while suffering, who feel strong on the outside but exhausted on the inside. Most of all, it is a reminder that depression may visit, but it does not get to stay, and it does not get to become your identity.

This book is not about perfection. It's about progress. It's about learning how to fight for your mind, your peace, and your future, one thought, one choice, and one day at a time.

Because as long as you have breath in your body, your story is not over, and you still have the power to kick depression in the butt.

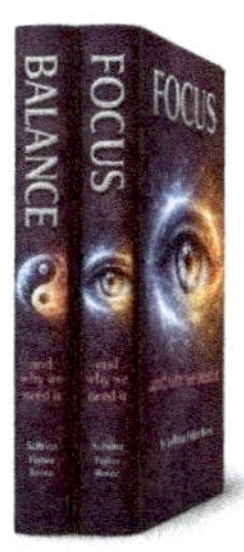

The Balance and Focus 2 Book Series

SaBrina Fisher Reece is the creator of the Balance and Focus Framework, a transformational approach to building emotional stability and disciplined clarity in everyday life. Through her books, speaking, and coaching, she teaches that balance is the foundation and focus is the force that shapes results. Her work helps individuals strengthen their inner world so they can build a more intentional and aligned life.

Blending spiritual awareness with practical structure, her work helps readers stabilize their internal world and direct their energy with intention.

She helps individuals cultivate emotional steadiness, mental discipline, and intentional living in every area of life.

Get Both Books Here:
https://mybook.to/TheBalanceFocusSeries

God is Not a Man

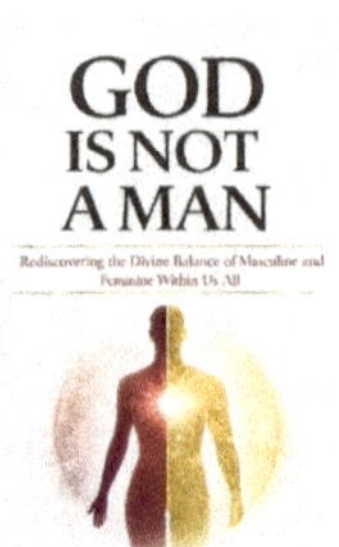

Is God exclusively male, or have we limited the image of the divine through tradition and culture?

In *God Is Not a Man: Rediscovering the Divine Balance of Masculine and Feminine Within Us All*, SaBrina Fisher Reece explores a powerful and often overlooked truth: divine source is not confined to gender. Drawing from scripture, ancient wisdom, global spiritual traditions, personal travel experiences, and modern psychological insight, this book challenges inherited assumptions while honoring faith.

Reece takes readers on a journey through Egypt, Greece, Indonesia, and Peru in search of a deeper understanding of God. Along the way, she examines universal law, the balance of masculine and feminine energy, and the spiritual maturity required to hold faith without limiting it. With clarity and conviction, she reveals how imbalance in our understanding of divine image has shaped theology, identity, and culture.

This book offers healing for women who have felt spiritually secondary and freedom for men who have felt pressured to suppress emotional depth. It speaks to the seeker who longs for truth without abandoning reverence. It affirms that strength and tenderness, authority and compassion, structure and intuition are not opposites but complementary expressions of one infinite source.

Rather than rejecting tradition, *God Is Not a Man* expands it. Rather than attacking faith, it deepens it. Readers will come away empowered, grounded, and more comfortable in their own wholeness, understanding that divine image is far greater than any single label.

For those ready to move beyond limitation and into balance, this book offers clarity, humility, and spiritual confidence.

Mind is All

In Mind Is All: Manipulating Ideas in a New Direction, SaBrina Fisher Reece explores the mechanics of thought-how ideas form, how they gain power, and how they quietly shape decisions, behavior, and belief. This book focuses less on positivity as a concept and more on mental leadership: learning how to consciously guide thought before it guides you.

Rather than motivating through inspiration alone, this book challenges readers to examine where their attention goes and why. It offers a framework for recognizing habitual thinking and deliberately steering it in a new, more constructive direction.

In this book, you'll learn how to:

Identify ideas that limit your growth
Redirect mental momentum instead of fighting it
Strengthen focus and internal discipline
Replace unconscious reactions with intentional thought
Use awareness to influence outcomes and decisions

Mind Is All is about reclaiming authority over your inner world. When you learn how ideas are formed and sustained, you gain the ability to reshape them-and in doing so, reshape your experience of life.

This book is for readers ready to think differently, not just feel better.

Pressure Down Plates Up

High blood pressure does not mean giving up flavor.

It does not mean bland food, boring meals, or feeling restricted at the dinner table. It means learning how to cook smarter, season differently, and nourish your body in a way that supports your heart.

In *Pressure Down Plates*, you will discover delicious, satisfying meals designed to help lower blood pressure naturally-without sacrificing taste. This cookbook focuses on simple ingredients, practical swaps, and flavorful combinations that make heart-healthy eating feel enjoyable instead of overwhelming.

Inside you'll find:

Low-sodium meals packed with flavor

Smart seasoning alternatives that don't rely on excess salt

Simple recipes for busy weeknights

Wholesome ingredients that support heart health

Easy dishes the whole family will love

Whether you are newly diagnosed, managing long-term hypertension, or simply wanting to be proactive about your health, this book gives you meals you can actually look forward to eating.

Taking care of your heart should feel empowering-not limiting.

Lower the pressure. Lift your plates. Enjoy your food again.

The World Is Ready (Ebook)
A Gentle Awakening to Sound, Energy, and the Spiritual Self is a compassionate invitation for those who sense there is more to life than what they were taught to see, yet still wish to honor their faith, their upbringing, and their reverence for God.

Written for readers raised within structured religious traditions, this book offers a safe and respectful bridge into spiritual practices that support balance, healing, and inner awareness. It reassures the reader that exploring sound healing, breathwork, meditation, grounding, and energy awareness is not a betrayal of faith, but a natural expansion of it.

Through deeply personal experiences, including recovery from major surgery supported by sound, private sound healing sessions, and sacred encounters in spiritual sites across the world, the author gently illustrates how ancient practices and modern understanding meet. From binaural beats and tuning forks to healing crystals, chakras, breath as life force, and the quiet power of the mind, each chapter unfolds with warmth, clarity, and emotional honesty.

This book does not preach, persuade, or pressure. Instead, it speaks softly to the soul, honoring curiosity while dissolving fear. It recognizes that spirituality does not belong to one religion, culture, or language, but lives within the shared human experience of seeking peace, connection, and meaning.

The World Is Ready is for anyone who has ever felt drawn to spiritual exploration but hesitated out of loyalty, doubt, or uncertainty. It affirms that spiritual practices are not witchcraft or rebellion, but tools of awareness that help us return to balance, regulate the nervous system, and remember our true nature.

This is not a call to abandon belief.

It is an invitation to remember who you are.

The world is ready.

Take A Breath With Bri

What if the one thing you've been doing your entire life... is the one thing you've never truly learned to do?

You breathe every single day. Over 20,000 times. Yet most of those breaths happen unconsciously, shallow and rushed, mirroring a world that rarely slows down.

In *Take a Breath With Bri*, motivational speaker Bri Reece invites you to rediscover the most powerful, accessible tool you already possess: your breath.

For decades, Bri lived a fast-paced life, running a business for over thirty years without ever pausing to understand the importance of intentional breathing. It wasn't until her fifties that she slowed down long enough to realize that breath is more than survival. It is regulation. It is clarity. It is peace. It is power.

Blending science, spirituality, and personal experience, this uplifting and deeply personal guide explores:

The medical benefits of slow, controlled breathing

How breath regulates anger, anxiety, and emotional overwhelm

Why impulsive reactions can destroy lives - and how one conscious breath can prevent it

Ancient breathing wisdom from Egypt, India, Tibet, the Andes, and beyond

Simple, practical breathing exercises you can begin immediately

How to teach children emotional regulation through breath

The spiritual significance of breath as the life force within us all

Each chapter gently reminds you that before reacting, before speaking, before escalating, you can pause and take one intentional breath.

Bri's signature message, "Take a breath with Bri, and you will see that everything will be all right," has helped thousands regulate their emotions and find calm in moments of chaos. Now, through this book, she teaches you how to create that steadiness for yourself - anytime, anywhere.

This is not a medical manual. It is a life manual.

It is for the parent who wants to model calm.

It is for the young person overwhelmed by anxiety.

It is for the individual who reacts too quickly.

It is for the spiritual seeker.

It is for anyone who is tired of living in survival mode.

Before you reach for anger. Before you reach for pills. Before you reach for regret. Reach for your breath, and watch your life change - one inhale at a time.

www.ingramcontent.com/pod-product-compliance
Lightning Source LLC
LaVergne TN
LVHW010904110826
845149LV00005B/1466

* 9 7 8 1 9 7 1 6 2 2 7 1 2 *